P9-CFA-862

BEYOND VOCATIONAL EDUCATION

CAREER MAJORS, TECH PREP, SCHOOLS WITHIN SCHOOLS, MAGNET SCHOOLS & ACADEMIES

David J. Pucel

EYE ON EDUCATION
6 DEPOT WAY WEST, SUITE 106
LARCHMONT, NY 10538
(914) 833–0551
(914) 833–0761 fax
www.eyeoneducation.com

Copyright © 2001 Eye On Education, Inc.
All Rights Reserved.

For information about permission to reproduce selections from this book, write: Eye On Education, Permissions Dept., Suite 106, 6 Depot Way West, Larchmont, NY 10538.

Library of Congress Cataloging-in-Publication Data

Pucel, David J.
    Beyond vocational education : career majors, tech prep, schools within schools, magnet schools, and academies / by David J. Pucel.
    p.   cm.
    Includes bibliographical references.
    ISBN 1-930556-04-7
    1. Vocational education—United States. 2. Career education—United States. 3. School-to-work transition—United States. I. Title.

    LC1045.P77 2001
    373.01'13—dc21

                                                                00-055154

10 9 8 7 6 5 4 3 2

Editorial and production services provided by
Richard H. Adin Freelance Editorial Services
52 Oakwood Blvd., Poughkeepsie, NY 12603-4112
(845-471-3566)

TABLE OF CONTENTS

ABOUT THE AUTHOR

David J. Pucel is Professor and Coordinator of the Office of Professional Development Outreach for the Department of Work, Community, and Family Education at the University of Minnesota. A recent President of the American Vocational Education Research Association, he has authored or co-authored four major books on career and technical education curriculum and contributed chapters to four others. He has worked closely with the Southern Regional Education Board, schools in Minnesota and Canada, and state departments in four states to revitalize vocational education.

PREFACE

PURPOSE OF THIS BOOK

The primary purpose of this book is to provide a rationale, model, and procedures for implementing change in high schools. Specifically, it focuses on the adoption of applied, context-based, and community-based education aimed at eliminating the competition between academic and vocational education and promoting cooperation in creating career-based education. It presents career-based education as a common element within many of the current high school reform formats such as career major programs, Tech Prep, schools within schools, magnet schools, academies, and school-to-work.

WHAT YOU WILL GAIN FROM THIS BOOK

This book will provide you with a rationale, procedures, and examples for understanding and/or implementing the following and much more.

- Career major programs
- Tech Prep
- Schools-within-schools
- Academies
- Magnet schools
- School-to-work
- Community-based education
- Mentoring
- Shadowing
- Internships
- Career courses
- Context-based education
- Integrated instruction
- Articulated instruction
- Applied instruction 2+2 programs
- 2+2+2 programs
- Performance-based instruction
- SCANS
- New American High School
- Technical education
- Portfolio evaluation

INTERNAL ORGANIZATION OF THE BOOK

The first chapter provides an accounting of how applied, context-based, community-based education has evolved and a rationale for why it has again become a central focus of educational reform. Chapter 2 presents an overview of the different school reform formats that are based on these elements (career majors, Tech Prep, school-to-work, magnet schools, and academies). Beginning with Chapter 3, the reader will find actual proven procedures along with examples for developing and implementing the new reform formats. Those readers already familiar with why such reforms are now being called for might want to go directly to Chapter 2. Those readers familiar with the differences and similarities between the various school reform formats might want to go directly to Chapter 3.

RATIONALE FOR THE TRANSFORMATION OF VOCATIONAL AND ACADEMIC EDUCATION

The reform of high schools to make them more relevant to the current and future needs of students is a national priority. High school vocational education programs of the past are now being asked to change their focus from specific occupational preparation to broader preparation for careers. A major verification of this movement has been the change in the name of the long standing American Vocational Education Association to the Association for Career and Technical Education. With the refocusing of high school vocational education programs on career education, specific occupational education has increasingly become the domain of technical education programs within postsecondary institutions. Academic programs are also being asked to change. Academic instructors are being asked to demonstrate the relevance of what they are teaching using applied teaching methods while helping students to develop rigorous academic skills. These changes in expectations for both vocational and academic programs have created an environment within which to re-think the goals of high schools and the relationships between academic and career education programs.

Most of us now realize that the Phillips Curve underlying supply and demand economics is no longer considered to be an adequate model of the new economy. We also realize that Taylorism, which promoted highly directive management practices and little employee involvement in decision-making, is no longer considered to be the optimal philosophy for managing organizations. Similarly, many are now beginning to realize that breaking the high school curriculum into college preparatory, vocational education, and general education programs is no longer considered to be an appropriate model for organizing high school programs. Society has changed from the industrial age, to the information age, and now to the knowledge/imagination age. These changes have not only had an impact on our economy, but they are also having a major impact on schools. High schools are now being challenged with preparing students with skills beyond abstract academic and highly procedural occupational skills. Society is now expecting all students to:

- ◆ Be able to creatively solve problems;
- ◆ Be able to apply what they learn to their future lives and work;
- ◆ Have a rigorous background in academic skills;
- ◆ Develop generalized employability skills;
- ◆ Explore and become technologically literate in potential careers; and
- ◆ Develop visions of their futures and how their education's can contribute to those visions.

Society is also expecting that the delivery format for education will be stimulating and relevant to students, so most, if not all students will feel their education is sufficiently worthwhile and relevant to take school seriously and to stay in school until graduation.

The TRANSFORMATION MODEL

This book provides a rationale, model, and set of procedures for organizing high schools and delivering instruction capable of accomplishing these desired goals. It also focuses on achieving the goals for the New American High School established by the U.S. Department of education. The central theme is to organize schools around relevant career majors and to deliver integrated career and academic instruction using applied learning methodologies. This theme is currently being manifested within a variety of evolving school formats such as: career major programs, Tech Prep programs, academies, and magnet schools. The processes presented have proven to be successful in implementing each of these school formats. They move from establishing career majors, to developing courses, to incorporating appropriate community-based experiences, to integrating and articulating the programs, to evaluating program success using a set of criteria consistent with current expectations.

The model was developed and tested over a seven-year period. It has been presented at many Southern Regional Education Board (SREB) staff development sessions. It has been presented to state department officials in Alabama, Minnesota, West Virginia, and Pennsylvania. More than 1000 teachers have successfully participated in workshops using the model to modify their course syllabi.

The model has been so successful that the author was invited as the sole U.S. representative, along with one from the United Kingdom and one from Japan, to advise the Taiwan Ministry of Education on revising their high schools for the future. He was also invited to present the model to the Ministry of Education in Beijing, China, and to teachers in Canada.

Throughout the book reform initiatives are presented as a series of progressive innovations. Often schools cannot implement all reform innovations at one time. Therefore, schools opt to implement one or more innovations that are feasible within their current circumstances. Later they consider additional innovations.

The author would like to thank Dr. James Stone III, Associate professor in the Department of Work, Community, and Family Education at the University of Minnesota for his unselfish sharing of information, which has helped to format this book. He would also like to thank Dr. Gene Bottoms, Senior

Vice President of the Southern Regional Education Board and Director of the High Schools That Work initiative, for challenging him and allowing him to test the various models in workshops for teachers associated with his initiatives.

1

WHY APPLIED, CONTEXT-BASED, AND COMMUNITY-BASED HIGH SCHOOL REFORM?

This chapter provides a review of how applied, context-based, community-based education has evolved and a rationale for why it has become a central focus of educational reform. Those who are already familiar with why such reforms are desired, might go directly to Chapter 2. Chapter 2 presents an overview of a variety of current school reform formats that embrace these reform elements (e.g., career majors, Tech Prep, schools-within-schools, magnet schools, and academies). Those who are also familiar with the differences and similarities between the various school reform formats but want to know how to implement them might go directly to Chapter 3. Beginning with Chapter 3, the reader will find chapters containing proven procedures and techniques for implementing these new formats.

APPLIED CONTEXT-BASED AND COMMUNITY-BASED EDUCATION

Context-based education, simply put, is education within contexts that are viewed by students as relevant to their current and future lives. Often such contexts are career interests. Key characteristics of such education are providing examples of real-life applications of what is being taught, requiring students to apply what they are learning and to utilize it in problem solving, and having students participate in community-based experiences that draw upon what they are learning. Context-based education is not new. Historically it was the predominant form of education until the early 1900s. Historically people were educated in the context of a career while working alongside their parents or others who had mastered their career interests, and/or by receiving formal instruction from people who had experienced their career interests. For reasons discussed later in this chapter, context-based education gave way to discipline-based education during the early 1900s. Discipline-based education separated content into subject matter areas and treated the mastery of the subjects as the primary goal of education.

Applied context-based and community-based education is again being carried out within a variety of today's curriculum reform formats. Some of these formats are career major programs, Tech Prep programs, schools-within-schools, magnet schools, and academies. These formats are similar in some ways but different in others. Throughout this book, these and other formats are discussed along with examples of real schools in which they are being implemented. A list of the schools referred to throughout this book and information useful in contacting them is presented in the "Sample Schools" section at the end of this chapter. The schools include:

- ◆ St. Francis High School, St. Francis, MN, which has organized most of its curriculum around career majors;

- ◆ Baton Rouge Louisiana Magnet High School (http://brmhs.ebrps.subr.edu/body.html), which stresses visual and performing arts;

- ◆ Francisco Bravo Medical Magnet Senior High School (http://bravo-med42.lausd.k12.ca.us/), Los Angeles, CA, which stresses medical careers;

- ◆ Mohawk Valley Workforce Preparation Consortium (http://mohost.moric.org/stw/) located in the Mohawk Valley in upstate/central New York with a wide range of career programs that have significant community-based activities;

- ◆ San Diego High School Writing Academy (http://sdhs.sandi.net/writing_academy), which is a school-within-a-school, focused on writing careers;

- ◆ Minnesota Dakota County Tech Consortium (http://www.techprep.dctc.mnscu.edu/), which is a Tech-Prep consortium with a 4-year sequence of study culminating in a certificate or an associate degree in a technical career area;

♦ Massachusetts Academy of Mathematics and Science (http://www.massacademy.org/College Web), which is a public high school for students in grades 11 and 12 interested in careers in math and science; and

♦ Monmouth County High Technology High School (http://www.hths.mcvsd.k12.nj.us/), Lincroft, New Jersey, which is focused on high-tech careers.

Although these types of schools address context-based and community-based education around different contexts, they all have many elements in common and are driven by similar views of how education in the future should be conducted.

The desire to reform high schools in these directions is not only a United States phenomenon. This author was invited by the Taiwan Ministry of Education as the sole representative from the United States, along with one professor from the United Kingdom, and one from Japan to provide advice on the changing roles of vocational and academic education within their comprehensive high schools. He was also invited by the Central Educational Science Research Institute for China to make a similar presentation in Beijing. The need to adapt educational practices to current and future societal needs is being recognized around the world.

In addition to educational reform being driven by changes in society, reform is being driven by research on how students learn best. Educational research has shown that in a society where essentially the total population needs to be well educated, discipline-based education is not always effective. Large numbers of learners are not able to take content taught in an abstract fashion and apply it to their work and lives. They need to be taught in ways that make the application of what they are learning explicit, and they need to practice applying the content to real life situations. Research has shown that such education has an impact on motivating students are to learn. Students attend to things they feel are relevant and which they see as useful. Education which concentrates solely on the mastery of disciplines such as math, language arts, and science provides little motivation for students to learn.

Most students are concrete learners. In other words, they need to be shown how content applies and they need to be required to reflect on how it is applied. Herbart, one of the first learning theorists, wrote about this principle of learning as long ago as 1898 (Herbart, 1898). He pointed out that in order for a person to truly understand and be able to use information, the person must be able to integrate it into their "dome" of experience. In other words, a context that they understand and have experienced.

Researchers are also realizing that true problem solving is context based. They are finding that people cannot solve meaningful problems in creative ways unless they have knowledge of the context of the problem. Examples of problem solving can be given, and learning exercises can be presented, but true creative problem solving requires extrapolating and going beyond what is presented by drawing upon knowledge and experiences in imaginative ways. True problem solving has been found to be very much like invention. Invention usually takes place by taking existing ideas, knowledge, and things and using them creatively in new ways to solve a problem. For example, students cannot creatively solve an accounting problem with math unless they understand something about accounting. Students cannot creatively communicate their perceptions of the impact of technology in writing unless they know something about technology. Students may be able to complete well-constructed accounting exercises using math without understanding accounting, but that is not really creatively solving accounting problems. Students may be able to research what others have said about technology and report on it using language arts skills, but that is not creative thinking about technology problem solving. Rather, that is reporting on what others have creatively said based on others' understandings of technology and not those of the student. In other words, if the goal of educators is to truly teach students to creatively problem solve in real life and work, teaching students within contexts becomes essential.

Researchers have also found that many of the social, community, and career skills and understandings are difficult to abstract and teach in formal classrooms. They can be more effectively taught and reinforced by allowing students to experience real-life activities through community-based experiences. For example, providing a classroom description of how people interact within an office will not leave a student with the same level of understanding as spending time in an office and observing interactions.

Those associated with the sample schools mentioned earlier often attribute their success in helping students retain what they learn and being able to apply what they learn to the fact that their instruction is focused on the interests of their students. Within these schools, students have an opportunity to interact with other students with the same interests, which reinforces creative thinking. At an arts magnet school, students are not only taught relative to the arts but they interact with other students interested in the arts. This provides a focus for many discussions and intellectual contexts related to the arts.

Within the sample schools it is also recognized that developing a true understanding of the context of careers and the development of social skills surrounding those careers requires experiences beyond the school walls. Therefore, most have community-based experiences built into the curricula. For example, one of the health academies that will be described latter is located across the street from a medical center and requires each student to have an internship within the medical center.

CHANGING VIEWS ABOUT THE ROLE OF SCHOOLS

Since all of us went to school and we consider ourselves to be successful, why do schools need to change? The reason is that society has changed dramatically. Computers, the Internet, worldwide access to information through the Web, worldwide economies, just-in-time production procedures, robotics, and automated manufacturing are just examples of the environment within which current and future students will need to function.

These and other innovations are rapidly propelling us from the information age into what futurists are calling the knowledge/imagination age. In the knowledge/imagination age all individuals will not only be expected to possess information but they will be expected to be able to apply it to creative problem solving. The distinctions between workers who are to do what they are instructed to and the people who decide what they are to do are rapidly being eliminated. Quality circles, autonomous work cells, team decision making, continuous process improvement, ad hoc team management practices, and flattening of organizations, are just a few of the new innovations in the world of work that require all people to be educated in creative problem solving rather than just information accumulation. The list could go on and on. Decision-making skills and self-initiative are now being expected of all people, and educational practices need to be adapted so all students are well educated. The two basic questions facing educators and society are, "What will it mean to be well educated?" and "How can such education be provided to all students?" What is needed is a new vision of a quality high school education and how it might be delivered.

IMPLICATIONS FOR
CHANGING HIGH SCHOOLS

In response to current life and workplace requirements, the educational community within the United States has defined a new set of criteria for what it considers to be a quality American high school. A broad-based advisory group was assembled by the U.S. Department of Education to create criteria for the ideal American high school. Figure 1.1 lists those criteria.

FIGURE 1.1 CRITERIA FOR THE
NEW AMERICAN HIGH SCHOOL

- ◆ Help students achieve high levels of academic and technical skills.
- ◆ Teach students in the context of a career major or other special interest.
- ◆ Offer hands-on learning in classrooms, workplaces or community service.
- ◆ Access a wide range of career and college information.
- ◆ Prepare students for college and careers.
- ◆ Work with teachers in small schools-within-schools.
- ◆ Win the support of a caring community.
- ◆ Receive extra support from adult mentors.
- ◆ Benefit from strong links with postsecondary institutions.
- ◆ Use technology to enhance instruction and learning.

(*Vocational Education Weekly,* 6/3/96)

The group addressed the need for all students to achieve high levels of academic and technical skills. Notice that this includes technical skills as well as academic skills. It is envisioned that these goals will be accomplished by teaching students within the context of career majors or special student interests and providing students with community-based learning experiences beyond the school classroom as part of formal schooling. It also indicates that students should have hands-on experience with applying what they learned as well as intellectual experiences.

Society has reaffirmed that education should be functional and that students should be taught in contexts of personal interest. What has become apparent is that neither the abstract academic nor the highly procedurally oriented vocational education of the past is meeting the needs of modern society. What is needed is an educational model that can blend the two, in ways that (a) enable all students to learn rigorous academics in an applied manner within the context of careers, and (2) enable students to acquire sufficient amounts of hands-on skills associated with their careers, to be able to perform basic practices as a context for creative problem solving and further education. This goal currently underlies major curriculum reform movements within the United States such as Tech Prep, school-to-work, The New American High School, and Goals 2000. Each of these is described in Chapter 2. The emphasis on broad career education in high school and the deferring of specific occupational training until post-high school, is very evident in the fact that the American Vocational Association (AVA) recently changed its name to the Association for Career and Technical Education (ACTE). With this change has come the realization that the focus of career preparation in high schools should not be on direct entry into the world of work. It has changed to providing students with a broad-based understanding of the careers they are interested in and the development of basic occupational skills that will help them as they specialize in the future. Within this book, the term "career courses" will be used to reference this new vision of what many have considered to be vocational education. The new term is intended to go beyond the traditional concept of vocational education as being only relevant for those preparing for semi-skilled and skilled occupations. Within this context, career education includes any experiences students have that are designed to acquaint them with the occupational skills and understandings associated with their career interests. This includes those associated with unskilled, skilled, technical and professional careers. The development of such skills along with academic competencies is the underpinning of magnet schools, academies, Tech Prep programs, and school-to-work programs focused on any career.

The challenge for educators is to develop a revised curriculum and new methodologies for implementing that curriculum, which are consistent with these new expectations. The curriculum processes and models presented in this text address how to evolve current educational practices to meet the new societal requirements.

REALIGNING EDUCATIONAL PRACTICE WITH CURRENT SOCIETAL NEEDS

The following is a brief historical overview of the relationship between educational practice and changes in society as a backdrop against which to consider how current reform might take place. It then provides more information about factors in current society that have led to the recommendations for the new American high school. A review of the relationship between educational practice and the society within which education is to take place clearly indicates that education is seen as preparing students to function within a society. It is an institution designed to acclimate and prepare students to function as productive citizens within society. In some countries this acclimation process goes a step further in an attempt to match individuals with established societal needs. Throughout this book, the models presented are based on the belief that, within the United States, students should have self-determination and free choice regarding their career aspirations. Therefore, the educational systems should not attempt to formally match students with the needs of society. This issue is being highlighted because many educators from the United States, at times, look toward other countries such as Germany and Denmark for exemplary career preparation models. Looking at alternatives is always good but those alternatives then need to be evaluated in terms of the needs of a given society and its views of the relationships between individuals and societal needs.

So, how has educational practice changed with changes in society? Early anthropological evidence shows that as formal societies were formed, adults taught their children such skills as how to make tools, how to hunt, and how to interact with others, as a basis for dealing with their work, family and community roles. Most often this was done informally through children living alongside adults and learning to do what they did. The earliest accounts of formal education indicate it was a vehicle for preparing the elite for religious and government positions. These positions required groups of people to have common understandings of such things as dogma, social expectations, historical events, procedures for dealing with societal events, and the ability to record and interpret records. The classics were originally taught as a means of learning how humans interact and how to deal with moral dilemmas. They were not taught solely as abstractions to be memorized or as a basis for interesting conversation. As commerce evolved, other content essential to doing business evolved. This required the educational systems to expand to prepare people for even more vocations. Some of the earliest accounts of formal education for business describe how accounting was taught in ancient Sumaria in order to facilitate vocational pursuits. People had to be able to record and communicate business transactions in a commonly understood way. What we today call the academic subjects, were originally taught as a means to vocational ends and thus in a career context. Educational systems evolved, as society required them to allow society to function.

The basic model of apprenticeship-type training was the major format for the education of the populace until the late 1800s. It provided functional education within the contexts of work, family, and community. Mothers and fathers taught their daughters and sons necessary skills. Those who were preparing for careers different than those of their parents found situations where they could work and study alongside those practicing their desired careers. This not only provided motivation to learn, but it allowed students to see how what they were learning was functionally applied. Learning in context gave them the ability to think in terms of concrete problems that required creative problem-solving skills. This was often described as the ability to innovate in their fields.

With the demand for mandatory education of the populace, educators were faced with the challenge of educating large numbers of students interested in many different contexts at the same time. At the same time, the amount of information in all disciplines and professions continued to explode. The questions facing educators were: How can we teach students with so many different contextual interests in the same classrooms? and How can we teach the large amount of new content efficiently? Educators began to focus more on organizing and teaching the expanded content than on educating students to apply the content in context. Academic teachers such as mathematics, science, and language arts teachers began to see their primary instructional role as teaching their content. Efficiency of instruction was often used to justify this practice. How could the mathematics teacher be expected to teach students within the large variety of students' interests?

Teaching methodologies for academic courses evolved to focusing on teaching the disciplines as entities in themselves rather than as content that could be functionally related to students' future lives and careers. Information was presented within evolving taxonomies for organizing each of the academic disciplines and portions of a taxonomy were taught in different grades. The goal ensured that students would study the required information from each discipline before graduating.

As this educational format evolved, parents became less and less involved as a bridge between the education of their children and the needs of society. At the same time, educators knowledgeable about their content areas became less interested in how the education of individuals corresponded with their visions of the future. A student's program of study was developed around what they were thought to need rather than how it contributed to the student's life goals.

By the early 1900s the high school curriculum in most schools was divided into three overlapping but distinct programs, the college preparatory program, the vocational program, and the general education program. Education became formalized and for the most part was restricted to taking place in school classrooms. The college preparatory track was to provide an efficient abstract academic education in the arts, science, mathematics, and social sciences to prepare students for further study in college. The vocational track was assumed to require a less rigorous academic background and more education in the concrete skills associated with specific occupations. It was designed to prepare students for direct entry into skilled and unskilled occupations. By Federal law, it needed to concentrate on occupations requiring less than a baccalaureate education. The general track was assumed to generally prepare students for life with no specific focus (Conant, 1967). As the three-track system evolved, the academic and general curricula were no longer context-based. The vocational program was context-based but it was not designed to provide students with a rigorous foundation of academic skills and was limited to a specific range of occupations.

With the coming of the information age, the focus on students acquiring and accessing more information became even more pronounced. The vocational education programs within high schools became viewed as taking curricular space that could better be devoted to academics. The 1983 Carnegie report, *A Nation at Risk* (Carnegie Foundation, 1983) suggested that what was needed was to ensure all students developed rigorous academic skills. It ignored the roles vocational and practical arts education might play in helping students develop skills and understandings related to their career interests and in providing a context for context-based education.

Standardized achievement tests developed to assess achievement during high school have also reinforced abstract instruction and learning. Students receive scores that affect their futures based on how much information they acquire. The tests do not focus on if they can apply the information in creative ways in context.

This pattern of academic education continued as societies moved through the information age. Given that there was more information available, educators increasingly saw the need to more efficiently deliver that information, and themselves, as people who deliver content rather than helping students be able to see how the content is useful to their lives.

This goal of acquiring and conceptually understanding large amounts of information and being able to recall it in a context free environment has never been the primary goal of education. Therefore, instructional methodologies as they have evolved in high schools during the 1900s, have not been compatible with societal expectations. In 1918, educational leaders concerned about the lack of clear goals for education, argued that education should be directly related to preparing citizens for life and work. They included preparation for a "vocation" as a major goal of education. The seven cardinal principles of education, as presented in Figure 1.2, were developed as student outcome goals for education. The principles did not address how education should be delivered but its objectives.

FIGURE 1.2 SEVEN CARDINAL PRINCIPLES OF EDUCATION

1. Health
2. Command of fundamental processes
3. Worthy home membership
4. Vocation
5. Citizenship
6. Worthy use of leisure
7. Ethical character

   (Commission on the Reorganization of Secondary Education, 1918)

This concern for students being prepared for life and vocations was reaffirmed in the 1940s with the listing of "Ten Imperative Needs of Youth" by the Educational Policies Commission. That list of the imperatives is presented in Figure 1.3.

FIGURE 1.3 TEN IMPERATIVE NEEDS OF YOUTH

All youth need to:

1. Develop salable skills;
2. Develop and maintain good health;
3. Understand the rights and duties of citizenship;
4. Understand the significance of the family;
5. Know how to purchase and use goods and services intelligently;
6. Understand the methods and influence of science;
7. Develop capacity to appreciate beauty;
8. Know how to use leisure time;
9. Develop respect for others; grow in their insight into ethical values, and live and work cooperatively;
10. Grow in their ability to think rationally and express their thoughts clearly, read and listen with understanding.

(Educational Policies Commission, 1944)

Although the language was changed, the focus on preparing students for life and work continues to be the explicit goal of education. Recently, the Federal Congress again reviewed the goals of education and adopted Goals 2000. Those goals, presented in Figure 1.4, reaffirmed the need for students to be prepared for productive lives and employment.

FIGURE 1.4 AMERICA 2000 EDUCATION GOALS

By the year 2000:

♦ All children in America will start school ready to learn.

♦ The high school graduation rate will increase to at least 90 percent.

♦ Students will leave grades four, eight, and twelve, having demonstrated competency in challenging subject matter...so that they may be prepared for responsible citizenship, further learning, and productive employment.

♦ US students will be first in the world in science and math.

♦ Every adult will be literate and will possess the knowledge and skills necessary to compete in a global economy and exercise the rights and responsibilities of citizenship.

♦ Every school will be free of drugs and violence and will offer a disciplined environment conducive to learning.

(U.S. Department of Education, 1991)

These societal statements of educational goals and expectations clearly indicate that there has been a disconnect between educational practice in high schools and the societal expectations. The issue of whether schools should prepare students in rigorous academics is not in question. What these three sets of societal goals illustrate is the consistent belief that a major role of public education is to prepare students for functional life and work. The major goal of education is not to teach content. The issue then, is not if public schools should be engaged in preparing students with academics and for work, community, and family, but rather how.

THE CHALLENGE TO EDUCATION

As indicated earlier, educational institutions are being challenged because the public is becoming increasingly aware that students are not being taught to functionally apply what they learn in high schools. It is becoming clear that using college prep, vocational education, and general education as major organizers of high school programs is no longer effective. All high school programs should contain both academic and career components focused on the goals of students. This will require broadening the concept of career majors beyond those traditionally thought of as vocational education. Moving in this direction is apparent in the criteria for the New American High School.

Some changes are already taking place within the academic community. Changes in how academic subjects should be taught have been supported by major academic subject matter groups such as the National Council of Teachers of Mathematics (Kurtz et al., 1990), and the National Center for Improving Science Education (National Center for Improving Science Education, 1989). Both call for increased applied teaching, which requires teachers to relate what they are teaching to real-life applications in life and work. In addition, there have been major changes in high school expectations for vocational education.

IMPLICATIONS FOR CHANGING THE MISSION OF VOCATIONAL (CAREER) EDUCATION

Throughout the previous discussion, the role of academic education in high schools was questioned. Equally important is to question the role of vocational education in high schools. As the separation of discipline-based academic education and vocational education evolved, vocational education practices have also not kept up with societal expectations. During the industrial age, the focus of vocational education was on teaching the "how to" of occupations. Content was derived primarily by examining what people did in an occupation and then teaching others to do the same. Because vocational education by Federal definition was to prepare students for occupations requiring less than a baccalaureate degree, and the industrial age jobs of the time required primarily procedural skills, this made sense. However, it does not make sense today. Society has changed and the current expectation is that all students should be encouraged to have a broad-based education during high school and to defer occupationally specific preparation until after high school.

Vocational education practices, which were successful in satisfying the needs of the industrial age during the late 1800s and early 1900s, need to be questioned. Continuing them without adaptation will make high school vocational education obsolete as we continue into the knowledge/information age. For example, because preparation for direct entry into the world of work required substantial skill development, students in vocational courses tended to spend much of their time mastering increasingly complex occupational skills. This reduced the time available for them to develop academic competencies. Only related occupational academics began to be taught. This meant the only instruction vocational students received in math or language arts was that required to prepare them for their occupational interest. For example, carpentry students were taught carpentry math, and business students were taught business communications, rather requiring them to participate in rigorous math or language arts courses. Therefore, vocational students were not provided the range of skills most think are now needed in order to be successful in the future.

Vocational education for the industrial age was also founded on the premise that engineers and supervisors would make the primary decisions about what was to be done and how it was to be done, and that employees prepared in procedural skills were to carry out those decisions. Therefore, there was little instruction focused on problem solving and working in teams to consider and improve work processes.

Given the changed context of work, in 1991 the U.S. Secretary of Labor undertook an effort to identify generalizable skills required in most workplaces as a basis for preparing people for employment (U.S. Department of Labor, 1991). A broad-based committee of people from business, industry, and a wide variety of disciplines, was assembled to consider the skills that would be needed by all individuals who enter the workplace of the future. The list of skills, known as the SCANS skills (Secretary's Commission on Achieving Necessary Skills), are exemplary of those also developed by the Canadian government and the American Society for Training and Development. They are presented in Figure 1.5. The skills are divided into two portions. The first is a three-part foundation of skills that are considered to be needed in order to carry out the five major competencies.

FIGURE 1.5 SCANS SKILLS

◆ Three-part Foundation
- Basic skills: Reading, writing, arithmetic/ mathematics, listening, speaking
- Thinking skills: Thinks creatively, makes decisions, solves problems, visualizes, knows how to learn, and reasons
- Personal Qualities: Displays responsibility, self-esteem, sociability, self-management, integrity and honesty

◆ Five Competencies
- Resources: Identifies, organizes, plans, and allocates resources
- Interpersonal: Works with others
- Information: Acquires and uses information
- Systems: Understands complex inter-relationships
- Technology: Works with a variety of technologies

(U.S. Department of Labor, June 1991)

When one reviews these skills it is apparent that the Commission believed that students need a broad range of skills to be able to function in life and work, in addition to procedural skills associated with specific occupations.

Formal calls for the revision of vocational programs have occurred with the passage of the Perkins Act, which provided funds for Tech Prep (Brustein, 1993), and the School-to-Work Opportunities Act (Brustein, 1994). The Tech Prep movement called for the teaching of rigorous applied academics, along with authentic career competencies, organized around broad clusters of occupations relevant to a wide range of students. In order to receive Federal funds to support such programs, it required academic and vocational educators to work together to create an integrated curriculum around career majors. It also called for articulation of instructional programs between secondary and post-secondary institutions so students can make seamless transitions between high school and post-high school education, or into the work of work. Tech Prep is discussed in more detail in Chapter 2.

The school-to-work (STW) movement has encouraged schools to embrace the notion that all education does not take place within the school walls. It promotes community-based educational experiences which can assist students prepare for work. It also reinforced the notion that learning should be focused on preparing students for life and work through applied learning. The School-to-Work Opportunities Act established a National School-to-Work Office under the joint direction of the U.S. Departments of Labor and Education. In order to implement STW, schools are encouraged to establish partnerships with business and industry and community service agencies. These partnerships are to provide students with opportunities to spend a portion of their high school programs in real-world situations alongside people who are performing the actual type of work they hope to enter. In other words, the community-based experiences are like miniature apprenticeships. Implementing school-to-work is discussed in more detail in Chapter 6 under partnerships.

STW, as defined in the act, is a specific application of community-based experiences focused on a limited set of goals as specified in Federal law. Other more flexible applications of community-based experiences will be discussed later. As STW has been implemented, there has been a growing reaction from the public. Many feel it is somehow attempting to channel students into work slots within the economy that match the needs of business and industry to the detriment of individual student choice. Throughout this book the basic tenets underlying community-based experiences, applied learning, and revitalizing academic and vocational education are presented as bases for providing more meaningful opportunities for students and enabling them to have maximum flexibility in achieving their evolving personal goals and personal self-fulfillment. These basic tenets at times need to be separated from current specific legislative initiatives, which may include other agendas such as fulfilling the workforce needs of the country. Within this book, strategies for implementing community-based learning experiences, including STW, are presented in Chapter 6. They will be presented as ways of extending learning activities outside the classroom.

This writer has published a number of books over the years that have suggested modifications to vocational education that are compatible with changing societal needs. The first was in the early 1970s when the stress for adapting instruction to the needs of individuals became prominent. At that time a book entitled *Individualizing Vocational-Technical Instruction* (Pucel & Knaak, 1975), was co-authored with William C. Knaak. In 1989, he authored a book for McGraw-Hill on *Performance-Based Instructional Design* (Pucel, 1989). It was designed to present a methodology for developing instruction focused on developing performance capability. It is still used today as a text for technical trainers in business and industry and postsecondary technical college instructors. When it became apparent that vocational education in high schools and postsecondary schools needed to be differentiated in terms of purpose and methodology, a text entitled *Designing Challenging Vocational Courses* (Bottoms, Pucel,& Phillips, 1997), was co-authored with Gene Bottoms and Ione Phillips for the Southern Regional Education Board. That text was focused on designing vocational courses to enhance the development of academic competencies while developing career skills. This current book goes beyond the need to revise vocational education to the need to re-design high schools where academic and career education are equal partners in the development of students for their futures. It is a more comprehensive view of high school reform.

IMPLICATIONS FOR TEACHING METHODOLOGIES OF THE PAST AND PRESENT

As indicated earlier, although the educational goals of society have tended to remain relatively consistent over time, teaching methodologies have changed dramatically. Where the Sumarian merchant learned mathematics around being a merchant, mathematics now tends to be taught in an abstract manner with the primary goal of mastering mathematics. Curriculum development processes have tended to be driven by a reductionism philosophy. It has been viewed as more efficient to organize each discipline into a taxonomy of content representing a logical progression of mastering the discipline and then teaching that content. For example, originally writing was taught as a method of communicating. Communicating was the goal and writing was a tool. When writing became a discipline, curriculum began to focus on a taxonomy of the elements in writing. Separate books were published on grammar, sentence structure, parts of a letter, etc. Students were asked to take tests on each of these elements. The focus of instruction shifted to learning the elements. Therefore, although the focus on education being functionally related to what students will do after high school still existed in the stated societal goals of education, the instructional methodologies were not focused on those goals.

The reductionism philosophy was also applied to vocational education. Youth preparing for work prior to the 1900s worked alongside those practicing an occupation. As they did, they not only learned the procedural aspects of work in the context of real jobs but the social and ethical aspects. As technology became more complex, preparation for work became more formal. Work analysis procedures continued to develop to the point where taxonomies of skills required for each occupation were developed. These taxonomies focused on "task lists" containing lists of skills people perform with their hands. Few directly focused on decision-making or interpersonal interactions. As the focus shifted from doing real work to learning how to perform tasks, instructional procedures increasingly focused on teaching students to master each of the tasks. This was very similar to the way writing instruction shifted from teaching communication to teaching writing skills. The assumption was that students who had mastered the separate skills would be able to apply them to real work problems as needed.

As a result of the type of education described above, many students left school without the ability to apply what they had learned to life or work. Because students did not see relevance to life and work, many were not motivated to learn. They saw education as something imposed on them with little meaning. They were unable to take the academic abstractions they learned in school and generalize them to real world situations. Although they could more clearly see the relationship between vocational education skills and their futures, they were not able to problem solve and to clearly see how they could apply what was learned. This was not viewed as a serious problem as long as society needed only a relatively small portion of its citizens to be well- educated and problem solvers. Those who could take the abstractions and apply them to the real world were in sufficient numbers to fulfill the needs of society.

In our modern society, where essentially everyone must be educated and capable of applying their education to life and work, these teaching methodologies and perceptions of curriculum are no longer sufficient. If the new expectations are to be achieved, high schools can no longer just provide students with an abstract academic education and highly procedural industrial age vocational education. All students must participate in combinations of academic and career courses. The courses must be designed to provide students with a rigorous academic foundation and a broad range of skills related to their career interests. In other words, students should be expected to develop a wide range of skills such as those listed within the SCANS skills. In this process they must develop technological literacy related to their visions of their future lives and work. Technological literacy in a career area requires the possession of understandings of technological evolution and innovation in the area and the ability to apply tools, equipment, ideas, processes, systems, and materials (Pucel, 1994, 1995). Students must be taught how to create functional knowledge from what they learn in preparation for the coming of the knowledge/imagination age.

This can be accomplished by organizing the curriculum around career majors through high school structures such as career major programs, Tech Prep, academies, and magnet schools. The career majors in these schools must represent the full spectrum of career possibilities (professional, technical, and skilled) in which academic and career education are equal partners. Such majors can provide vehicles for context-based education, which will again facilitate the integration of what students learn into knowledge, which they can apply creatively to their future lives and work. This is the way education was done throughout most of history. It has also been the historically stated goal of education in the United States. However, it cannot be accomplished by simply going back to the exact methodologies used for teaching academic disciplines or vocational education in the near or distant past.

Therefore, throughout this book it will be shown that the commonly held assumption that vocational education has already achieved the desired applied, contextual, and community-based learning goals that are being set out for the rest of education is false. Vocational education is in just as much in need of major revision as any other program in the high school.

Although most would agree that such reform is being called for, the nature of the reform and how to accomplish it are not always clear. As President Clinton summarized, "We are now learning a lot more about learning and we know that a lot of people with very high intelligence levels learn better in practical settings. We also know that practical skills now require a higher order of thinking. So the old dividing line between vocational and academic is fast becoming blurred and will become more and more meaningless as time goes on." (National School-to-Work Learning & Information Center, 1996).

Figure 1.6 presents a visual summary of the concept underlying the required curriculum reform.

FIGURE 1.6 CONCEPT UNDERLYING CURRICULUM REFORM

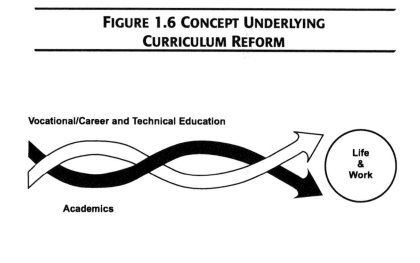

Within this model, both career education and academic education are seen as equal partners. Both have essential core content to be taught. This is an important concept as one considers reform. Career education is not just a context for the applied learning of academics. Also, the goal of high school career education is not to prepare students with a sufficient array of skills to the depth required to practice in an occupation. The goal of career education is to develop technological literacy within a student's career major as a context for meaningful/imaginative problem solving, and to allow students to experience realistic career activities as a basis for further education in the career area and for exploring their career interests in terms of their futures. Organizing the curriculum around career majors through different high school structures can allow educators to meet the current educational expectations of society while still providing students with a rigorous academic background. What is needed is a clear understanding of the alternative high school structures and the types of curriculum innovations that are possible within each. The rest of this text is devoted to developing that understanding.

REFERENCES

Bottoms, G., Pucel, D.J., & Phillips, I. (1997). *Designing challenging vocational courses.* Atlanta, GA: Southern Regional Education Board.

Brustein, M., (1993). *AVA Guide to federal funding for tech prep.* Alexandria, VA: American Vocational Association.

Brustein, M., (1994). *The school-to-work opportunities act: Overview.* Alexandria, VA: American Vocational Association.

Carnegie Foundation. (1983). *A nation at risk.* New York: Author.

Commission on the Reorganization of Secondary Education, U.S. Office of Education, (1918). *Cardinal principles of secondary education.* (Bulletin No. 35, 9). Washington, DC: U.S. Government Printing Office.

Conant, J.B. (1967). *The comprehensive high school.* New York: McGraw-Hill.

ED/DOE launch effort to reform high schools. *Vocational Education Weekly, 9* (8), 4.

Educational Policies Commission, National Education Association. (1944). *Education for all american youth* (pp. 225–226). Washington DC: The Association.

Herbart, J.F. (1898). *The application of psychology to the science of education.* (B. C. Mulliner, Trans.). New York: Charles Scribner's Sons.

Kurtz, V.R. (1990, October). NCTM standards. *School Science and Mathematics, 90*(6), 451–574.

National Center for Improving Science Education. (1989). *Science and technology education for the elementary years: Framework for curriculum and instruction.* Andover, MA: The Network.

National School-to-Work Learning and Information Center, U.S. Department of Education (1996, June). http://www.stw.ed.gov/factsht/fact5.htm. For additional information, please contact: The National School-to-Work Learning & Information Center, 400 Virginia Avenue, Suite 210, Washington, DC 20024, Phone: 1-800-251-7236, Fax: 1-202-401-6211

Pucel, D.J. & Knaak, W.C. (1975). *Individualizing vocational-technical instruction.* Columbus, OH: Charles E. Merrill. (ERIC No. 114 599, CE 005 463)

Pucel, D.J. (1989). *Performance-based instructional design.* New York: McGraw-Hill.

Pucel, D.J. (1994, Spring). Technological literacy: A critical requirement for all students. *School of Education Review, 6,* 32–42.

Pucel, D.J. (1995). Developing technological literacy: A goal for technology education. *The Technology Teacher, 55*(2), 35–43.

U.S. Department of Education. (1991). *America 2000: An eductational strategy.* Washington, DC, U.S. Department of Education, 34 pp., ED/OS91-13.

U.S. Department of Labor. (1991, June). *What work requires of schools: A SCANS report for America 2000.* Washington, DC: U.S. Government Printing Office.

SAMPLE SCHOOLS

♦ The Baton Rouge Louisiana Magnet High School
http://brmhs.ebrps.subr.edu/body.html
2825 Government Street
Baton Rouge, LA 70806

♦ The Francisco Bravo Medical Magnet Senior High School
http://bravo-med42.lausd.k12.ca.us/
1200 N. Cornwell Street
Los Angeles, CA 90033
Phone: (213) 342-0428

- The Mohawk Valley Workforce Preparation Consortium
  http://mohost.moric.org/stw/
  4937 Spring Road
  PO Box 168
  Verona, NY 13478-0168

- The San Diego High School Writing Academy
  http://sdhs.sandi.net/writing_academy
  1405 Park Blvd.
  San Diego, CA 92101
  Phone: 619/525-7455
  Fax: 619/231-0973

- The Dakota County Tech Consortium
  http://www.techprep.dctc.mnscu.edu/
  Dakota County Technical College
  1300 145th Street East
  Rosemount, MN 55068-2999
  Phone: (651) 423-8262
  Fax: (651) 423-8775

- St. Francis High School
  http://www.stfrancis.k12.mn.us/sfhs/sfhs_home. htm
  3325 Bridge St.
  St. Francis, MN 55070

- Mesabi East High School
  601 N. 1st St. W.
  Aurora, MN 55705

2

SCHOOL FORMATS AND HIGH SCHOOL REFORM INNOVATIONS

To accomplish the new high school reform goals, educators have developed a number of alternative school formats. Some of the major types are career major programs, Tech Prep, academies, schools within schools, and magnet schools. Each of them typically addresses the issues of applied, context-based, and community-based education in different ways. They each recognize the value of applied learning to enhance the meaningful learning of students. They each try and accommodate the need for a rigorous solid core of academic skills. Although all have an implicit career focus, some explicitly embrace the concept of career majors as the focal point of the applied learning. Some formats physically separate students into separate schools based on career interests, and others address the multiple career interests of different students within the same school. The term schools-within-schools does not actually refer to a specific type of format; it refers to the way the school curriculum is organized and presented to students. The term refers to programs that are viewed as distinctly separate from one another but which take place within the same overall school facility. Any of the other four types of formats listed above can be delivered as a school within a school if they have a large enough student body to warrant separate courses and separate management. The major difference from other programs offered in a school is that the schools within a school have substantially more curricular control. What follows is a brief description of each of the formats and some of the similarities and differences between them.

CAREER MAJOR PROGRAMS

Career major programs are combinations of existing courses within a high school that are recommended for students interested in a particular career cluster. Each of the other formats that will be discussed later also use career majors as a focal point for instruction. However, they go beyond just identifying a set of the regular high school courses that students might take if they are interested in a career.

The recommended programs of study for those interested in particular careers are used as counseling guides for course selection. There is no expectation that the courses will be integrated, or that there will be a body of students identified to be educated as a cohort. The career major program strategy can be used by a school to try to make a students' education more relevant without the need to make changes within the courses themselves. Such programs are not schools-within-schools nor do they meet the criteria for Tech Prep programs, academies or magnet schools.

An example of a school that has developed and counsels students around career major programs is St. Francis High School, St. Francis, MN, which is located in a semirural area near Minneapolis/St. Paul. It has been a model school in terms of recognizing the need for reform and providing instruction relevant to students' career interests. It also has Tech Prep programs. It has developed career major programs around potential student career pathways. Pathways are viewed as visions of how students might achieve their career goals. Those pathways include a Business Contact Pathway leading to managerial and sales careers; a Business Operations Pathway leading to office and clerical careers; a Social Services Pathway leading to educational and social services careers; an Arts Pathway leading to artistic, musical, and literary careers; a Technical Pathway leading to skilled trades and technical careers; and a science pathway leading to scientific and technical careers. Examples of these pathways are presented in Chapter 3. Currently available courses are recommended in different combinations to students depending upon their career interests.

Although this format does not go as far as some of the other formats presented, the fact that career major pathways are created and available to students is the first, and probably largest, giant step toward reform. This format is often used by smaller schools that are committed to reform goals but do not have the curricula resources to develop specialized curricula around career majors.

TECH PREP PROGRAMS

Tech Prep programs were described briefly in Chapter 1. Current federal legislation provides funding for Tech Prep programs focused on a prescribed range of technical career majors. Tech Prep career majors include technical preparation in at least one field of engineering technology; applied science; a mechanical, industrial, or practical art or trade; agriculture; health; or business. They are expected to contain both rigorous applied academic courses and career courses that lead to a certificate, an associate degree, apprenticeship, or direct employment. Career and academic courses are expected to be supportive of one another. The ultimate goal of Tech Prep programs is employment. Multiple Tech Prep programs typically occur within a comprehensive high school, a vocational high school, or a secondary vocational center, in cooperation with one or more postsecondary institutions. Tech Prep programs are to be planned and implemented through a consortium to ensure that cooperating high schools and postsecondary schools develop a joint plan and that instructional programs are focused on the current business and industry environment. The consortium contains one or more high schools and postsecondary institutions. It is advised by a committee of business and industry and community representatives. Each Tech Prep program should be designed to provide an articulated, seamless, non-duplicative program of studies, which allows students to transition from high school into the post-secondary institutions to complete their career preparation. The secondary and postsecondary institutions are actually expected to sign an articulation agreement that commits them to offering a joint program of studies with a non-duplicative sequence of classes and other experiences. Tech Prep planning guidelines formally recognize that it is the role of postsecondary institutions to provide the detailed technical training to prepare students for direct entry into the workplace. At times,

Tech Prep programs take the form of academies, if the academies meet the federal requirements.

An example of a Tech Prep consortium is The Dakota County Tech Consortium, located just south of Minneapolis/St. Paul. It provides a 4-year sequence of study culminating in a certificate or an associate degree. It offers programs in areas such as:

+ Sales Promotion/Advertising
+ Child Development
+ Culinary Arts
+ Computer Applications
+ Photography
+ Computer Repair

The consortium defines Tech Prep as follows:

> Tech-Prep education is an alternative to the college prep course of study. It prepares the student for a highly skilled technical occupation that allows either direct entry into the workplace as a qualified technician or continuation with further education leading to baccalaureate and advanced degrees. Tech-Prep is a 4-year sequence of study beginning in the 11th grade through 2 years of postsecondary occupational education culminating in a certificate or associate degree. Tech-Prep education is funded under two sections of the Carl D. Perkins Vocational and Applied Technology Education Act through grants to states that, in turn, fund local Tech-Prep efforts. Funding is available for in-service training for teachers to implement Tech-Prep education.

A Tech Prep program consists of one or more of the elements listed here.

- Leads to an associate degree or two-year certificate.

- Provides technical preparation in at least one (career) cluster.
- Builds student competence in math, science, and communications through a sequential course of study.
- Leads to employment placement.
- Through Articulation, links two years of high school in specific career clusters with two years of postsecondary from a technical or community college.
- Provides staff development opportunities.

(http://www.techprep.dctc.mnscu.edu/)

To communicate more effectively with others, the consortium has also developed a list of terms that are often used to describe Tech Prep as a basis for better understanding. These terms are defined throughout this book. The terms are:

- 2 + 2
- Articulation agreements
- 2 + 2 + 2 or 4 + 2 + 2
- Career clusters (majors)
- Shadowing
- Partnerships
- Internships
- Integrated curriculum
- Mentoring
- Work-based learning
- Career fields
- SCANS skills
- Portfolio assessment

Most Tech Prep programs include community-based experiences as part of the curriculum. In some cases, they are coordinated with federally funded school-to-work programs.

Academies

Academies are designed to provide instruction for a group of students focused on a particular type of content and/or a specific set of careers. For example, a science and technology academy, an international business academy, a technology and engineering academy, or a writing academy. Some academies formally state a goal of integrating instruction between the different subject matter courses. However, even if this is not a formal requirement, the fact that a group of students with the same interests is within the same class sessions tends to focus instruction within the context of relevant careers. For example, in a science and technology academy the focus will automatically be around the application of what is being learned. This increases the likelihood that instructors will teach in an applied manner, which, in turn, means they will relate what they are teaching to careers. Most academies also require students to take career courses and/or career related community-based experiences as part of the curriculum.

Academies may be physically separate schools, or schools within schools. They are not restricted to the career areas financed by Tech Prep legislation. To the extent that an academy includes authentic career applications of the content in academic courses and career courses aimed at developing a set of career skills, they are very similar to Tech Prep programs. In fact, academies that meet the Tech Prep funding criteria are also called Tech Prep programs. To the extent that academies are organized as physically separate schools with separate administrative staffs, they are very similar to magnet schools.

The Massachusetts Academy of Mathematics and Science (http://www.massacademy.org/CollegeWeb/) is an example of a stand-alone public high school academy for students in grades 11 and 12. It is a collaborative effort among the Commonwealth of Massachusetts, Worcester Polytechnic Institute (WPI), and the high schools of Massachusetts to identify and nurture the potential of students with exceptional aptitude for mathematics and science. Students in grade 12 attend classes at WPI as part of their high school curriculum. The academic performance of students is assessed in a wide variety of ways including written tests, portfolios, student presentations, individual and group projects, and classroom participation. These activities require students to integrate and reflect on what they are learning within the academic and career foci of the academy. Each academic year, every Academy student must complete 56 hours of documented, supervised community service. As one examines the types of activities students are expected to engage in, it is apparent that the academy is focused on career majors.

The San Diego High School Writing Academy is an example of a school-within-a-school academy. It supports the general writing curriculum for the entire school and a Writing Center for a group of students interested in writing as a career. The academy offers writing classes, writing workshops, and prepares publications. The Writing Center has a staff of Writer's Assistants who are trained to aid students in all stages of the writing process. Student programs include writing classes and journalism, a variety of writing workshops, experiences writing a monthly writing newsletter, the school newspaper, and an international publication produced with sister schools in Argentina, Austria, and Russia. By the nature of the applied expectations of this academy, it has a focus on writing as a career major.

Notice that both of these academies address career majors that go beyond those traditionally associated with vocational education.

MAGNET SCHOOLS

Magnet schools are very similar to academies, but they are typically, physically separate schools with a separate administration. Like academies, their curricula are focused on particular content areas and/or career clusters. Magnet schools typically receive separate financing from and serve a wider geographic area than the area immediately surrounding the school. At times, they may be a school district-wide magnet or a state magnet. As with academies, they have separate student groups interested in the particular focus of the magnet. Because they have a large, separate, homogeneous population of students, faculty can focus instruction on how content can be applied to career contexts. Magnets tend to be most able to develop jointly planned and executed integrated curricula. That is because all students in the school have interests in the same specialization and instructors are expected to relate what they teach to that specialization. Magnets have been established in many career areas.

The Baton Rouge Louisiana Magnet High School stresses visual and performing arts. It was selected as an Outstanding Secondary School by the National Commission on Excellence in Education. The school's visual and performing arts programs include choral, dance, drama, instrumental music, piano, radio, television, and visual arts programs. It has a television studio where live television broadcasts are made and broadcast. It has two radio stations and a mini-theater. Students apply what they learn through art exhibits, concerts, plays, ballets, recitals, radio and television shows, and musical theatre productions. Therefore, students are asked to develop a set of career skills and demonstrate them as they complete the curriculum.

The Francisco Bravo Medical Magnet Senior High School is located in Los Angeles, CA. Though a magnet with various specialized programs, Bravo is also a comprehensive high school, ninth through twelfth grade. The school is located across the street from the University of Southern California (USC) Health Science Campus and the USC/County General Hospital (LAC). As a magnet, the majority of the student body arrives by bus from all areas within Los Angeles Unified School District. The student population is very diverse: 11.3% African American; 17.7% Asian; 16.6% Caucasian; 45.6% Latino; 0.2% Native American; 0.3% Pacific Islanders; and 8.2% Filipino. Career options include medical lab assistant, medical microbiology, nursing assistant/medical terminology, and ophthalmologic technician. Each student has an on-site clinical experience in a lab at USC+LAC Medical Center and participates in an inter-disciplinary plan with an English and science teacher. Experiences in the biological labs allow students to develop practical and academic skills in preparation for a career in the health sciences.

Again, notice that both of these magnets, as well as the academies, tend to address career majors that go beyond those traditionally associated with vocational education. They are examples of the expansion of the career major concept into what have traditionally been called the professions. Yet, they are expected to have the same instructional methodology models as Tech Prep. They are focused on career majors, they tend to have an integrated curriculum around the majors, they often have community-based experiences, and students are expected to develop specific skills and understandings associated with the career majors.

Each of the major formats is a vehicle for implementing one or more of the applied, contextual, community-based curricular innovations. All are based on developing instruction around career majors, whether the students choose a set of courses from those already available in the high school, or if specialized courses are designed and offered for their major.

CURRICULAR INNOVATIONS

Each of the four reform formats discussed earlier can be implemented in a variety of ways depending upon the particular set of curricular innovations to be included during their execution. For example, an academy could use existing courses, taught as they have been in the past, or it could require instructors teaching academy courses to teach around problems arising from the career majors of the academy. The same academy could develop an articulated program of studies with an associated postsecondary institution, or it might not. Students might be required to participate in community-based experiences, or they may not. Students might attend courses as a group, or they may not.

When thinking about adopting and evaluating programs aimed at reform, one needs to consider the extent to which the program includes or excludes eight major curricular innovations. The number adopted indicates the extent to which the reform approximates meeting the applied, contextual, community-based goals of the New American High School. Whether specific innovations are included or not is often determined by what is practical and doable at a given point in time, in addition to educational philosophy. The size of a school, its remoteness, its financial situation, and its proximity to postsecondary institutions are examples of factors that might impact decisions. The innovations are presented in Figure 2.1. It is assumed that each subsequent innovation includes the characteristics of those preceding it, therefore, eliminating the need to repeat the discussion of those characteristics. The first three innovations are variations of applied instruction.

FIGURE 2.1 INNOVATIONS

- ◆ Applied Instruction
  - Teaching around applied examples
  - Including applied learning exercises
  - Including applied problem solving
- ◆ Career Majors
  - Advising around career majors
  - Teaching in the context of student majors
  - Developing an integrated curriculum
- ◆ External Relationships
  - Requiring community-based experiences
  - Articulating the curriculum with postsecondary institutions

---

APPLIED INSTRUCTION

The first set of three innovations can be accomplished without establishing career majors. They can be accomplished by changing the instructional methodologies instructors use within their existing classes. They are gradations of changing the instructional methodology from focusing only on the discipline being taught, to real world applications of the content. They in no way are meant to compromise the actual content being taught, they are only different ways of presenting the content. Although adopting these innovations alone will not result in an instructional program that meets the expectations of the New American High School, they will represent a major step in moving from discipline-based to applied instruction. The major element that would still be missing is the focusing of the applications on a specific context. It is when schools venture into innovations that require planning around career or special interest contexts that they can really achieve the new expectations.

TEACHING AROUND APPLIED EXAMPLES

This is the easiest curricular innovation to adopt because the only instructional change required is for instructors to provide examples of how what they are teaching is actually used in real life. Many instructors have been doing this for years. This assists with student motivation and demonstrates the relevancy of the content. The major drawbacks of stopping with this innovation alone are that it does not require students to actually apply the content and oftentimes the examples are episodic. Episodic means that the examples come from a wide range of unrelated settings and not around a consistent context of interest to the student.

INCLUDING APPLIED LEARNING EXERCISES

This innovation is usually added to the teaching around applied examples described above. It requires instructors to go beyond providing examples to having students actually apply what they are learning to real career or life activities through exercises. For academic instructors this adds the burden of creating meaningful application exercises and judging the adequacy of the applications of the content to career or life activities. Career course instructors, by the nature of their courses, typically do this.

Many of the currently available applied learning materials have adopted this level of applied learning. For example, the applied academic series produced by the Center for Occupational Research and Development (CORD) in Waco, Texas, is often used within Tech Prep programs. The materials are developed to show students where the academic content can be applied, and there are applied learning exercises. The exercises contain prescribed procedures for completing them and already pre-determined solutions.

Although this approach is another major step in terms of making instruction relevant to students, it still has major drawbacks. First, given that it tends to be used with highly prescribed exercises, it does not require creative problem solving. Second, the focus is on showing and requiring an application and not a set of applications around a particular career major. Therefore, applications tend to be drawn from episodic areas of convenience and are not cohesively focused on a career major.

INCLUDING APPLIED PROBLEM SOLVING

Requiring applied problem solving is differentiated from applied learning exercises because it requires that application activities be designed to require creative problem solving. As indicated above, applied learning can take place through highly structured learning exercises where the students only need to complete steps 1 to 10 to get the correct answer. This provides students with experience applying the content. For example, students could be presented an example on how to calculate the size of a window on a sheet of paper where all of the information is presented and all the student has to do is complete the calculations. This satisfies the requirement of an applied learning exercise because students had to apply the content. However, it does not require creative problem solving if students are not required to make judgments about what to do. For example, rather than providing the figures that need to be calculated, students might be presented with the goals the window is to accomplish within the building. They could then be required to research the sizes that would be needed to satisfy those requirements and then do the calculations. This innovation should not be confused with formats where students determine what they will study. This format requires students to eventually be able to apply content as required in the course (e.g., algebra, composition, accounting, carpentry) to real problems in a creative way rather than to just complete instructor designed exercises.

This method of applied learning is particularly compatible with the adoption of career majors. After completing the instruction around the content to be taught, students could be asked to identify a situation within their career majors where the content is relevant. They could further be asked to present their problems and solutions to the instructor and/or the class. This rather simple type of assignment brings the application of what is being taught to a new level. It requires students to actively reflect on what is being taught in the context of their majors. This should not only be more motivating, but it should increase the likelihood that students will integrate the new content within their long-term knowledge bases for use in the future.

CAREER MAJORS

Student learning through applied learning methodologies can be greatly enhanced if that learning takes place in reference to a relatively consistent context that is important to the student. Therefore, the adoption of career majors as a way of projecting and organizing the curriculum is an important addition to achieving applied, context-based education. As was pointed out in Chapter 1, creative problem solving is now recognized to be context-based and cannot be effectively taught within a context-free environment. When going the next step beyond applied instructional techniques to acknowledging and/or actually developing career majors, a school is acknowledging the desirability of context-based education.

ADVISING AROUND CAREER MAJORS

Advising around career majors can be done in reference to combinations of typical existing courses within a high school and/or unique courses designed for the major. The basic requirement for such advising is that combinations of recommended courses be developed around clusters of careers. In its simplest form, career majors of interest to the students are identified. Then teams of instructors determine which combination of courses would be most reasonable for students interested in those majors. During advising, students are presented a list of majors and lists of recommended courses for each major as vehicles for decision making. Again, in its simplest form this innovation requires no actual change in the courses or in the way the courses are taught. It just acknowledges that students should seriously think about their future careers and how to get there. Examples of how to plan such majors and courses within them are presented in Chapter 3. A sample of materials that are helpful to students who wish to explore their career interests was developed by the Mohawk Valley Workforce Preparation Consortium, located in the Mohawk Valley in upstate/central New York, and are presented at the end of Chapter 6.

As indicated earlier, the St. Francis High School has developed a set of career majors along with the courses that would be most appropriate for preparing for those careers. Mesabi East High School in Aurora, MN has also developed such career majors and provides lists of specific careers that require 1 to 3 years of postsecondary education and 4 years of education beyond high school for each of their career majors. Examples are provided in Chapter 3 on developing career majors.

TEACHING IN THE CONTEXT OF STUDENT MAJORS

Once majors have been developed, the next step is teaching within the context of those majors. As indicated above, it is possible to develop majors composed of existing courses and have the instructors teach them the way they always have. Although that is a major step forward from having no majors, it does not maximize the educational power of majors. Instruction using applied learning methods within the context of career majors is recommended. When teaching within the context of a major, each student is asked to relate and apply what is being taught in each of their courses to that major. This does not mean instructors should completely change their instructional methodologies for presenting their content. It means adding a couple of components to their methodology. If this innovation is adopted, each instructor would be asked to require each student to apply what they are learning to their career major context. This type of assignment is usually given after they have mastered the content being taught. For example, a student interested in going into business would be expected to provide examples of how what they are learning can be applied to business. They might also be asked to show how real problems within business are solved using what they were studying. The key is that, in each class, students would always be required to reflect on the content in reference to their current career aspirations. Students might change their interests over time and that is all right, however, during a given period of time they would focus on their current interest. The advantage of this approach is that students will be forced to integrate what they are learning into a consistent context, which will give them a higher likelihood of developing problem solving abilities in those areas. The argument for problem solving being context-based was presented in Chapter 1.

DEVELOPING AN INTEGRATED CURRICULUM

With the incorporation of career majors into the curriculum, sets of courses appropriate for students pursuing each career major would have been identified. So far, the instructional innovations within classrooms have been addressed in terms of the individual teachers within their classrooms. Developing an integrated curriculum is an innovation that requires joint planning and teaching across the courses within the major. Integration can take place between two or more courses in the major. In the example from the Francisco Bravo Medical Magnet Senior High School presented earlier, each student has an on-site clinical experience in a lab at USC+LAC Medical Center and participates in an interdisciplinary plan with an English and science teacher. Delivering such instruction requires joint planning between institutions and teachers; and competencies that students are expected to develop within each institution or class must be identified. Then the instruction within each must be jointly planned and orchestrated to reinforce one another around the career interest. How this is done is presented in Chapter 4.

A truly integrated curriculum is designed so the academic and career competencies being taught at any given time reinforce one another, and students are required to apply all the content they are learning to their career area. As will be shown later during the designing of instruction, this is a difficult goal to achieve. Oftentimes an integrated curriculum is only implemented with a subset of courses within a major.

EXTERNAL RELATIONSHIPS

REQUIRING COMMUNITY-BASED EXPERIENCES

Community-based instruction takes place in the community outside the walls of the school. It must be formally planned as part of the total curriculum. Such experiences allow students to again have interaction with adults who practice in their career areas, as students did prior to the adoption of formal schools. Students can experience the way things are actually done in the real world and the environment within which a career takes place.

There are may forms of community-based instruction ranging from shadowing, where a student is asked to accompany a person to observe what they do, to formal apprenticeship where a person is expected to learn skills and to actually perform real work. Community-based instruction should not be confused with work experience or work release programs where the primary goal is income or general work activity. Community-based instruction is designed to supplement in-school instruction and is always planned with clear learning expectations.

Most teachers can accomplish some form of this innovation relatively easily. Teachers can simply ask students to interview people for a specific purpose designated by the instructor. For example, in a math class, when ratios are being discussed, students could be asked to arrange an interview with a person in their career area to get examples of how ratios are applied. Things get more complicated if learning expectations require some form of actual work in a community-based environment. This requires that teachers or other authorized personnel within the school develop learning plans in the form of contracts. The plans are usually developed between the teacher, the student, and the actual supervisor in the community site. They include what the student is to experience and when and how the experience will be evaluated. How to actually implement community-based alternatives, along with examples, are provided in chapter 6.

ARTICULATING THE CURRICULUM WITH POSTSECONDARY INSTITUTIONS

So far, the innovations have dealt with things that can be planned solely by high school personnel. However, there is increasing concern for coordination between high school and postsecondary programs. As society has become more complex, most students will need to have some postsecondary as well as secondary education. In order for the transition from high schools to postsecondary institutions to be most efficient, there is a call to reduce the redundancy between courses taken in high school and in postsecondary institutions. The joint curriculum planning process between high schools and postsecondary institutions in order for students to experience a smooth and seamless transition from high schools to postsecondary programs is called articulation. Articulation is a major component of Tech Prep programs as indicated earlier in this chapter. Further information on the development of articulation agreements is presented in Chapter 5.

THE IDEAL

The ideal educational reform would be to develop a curriculum that is applied, contextual, community-based, integrated, and articulated, which fosters problem solving within the context of career majors. However, that is difficult to implement. Particularly, if people with multiple career interests are being taught together in the same classes at the same time. The problems that were highlighted in Chapter 1 that have led to a focus on disciplines rather than applications loom large. In order to try and manage programs, compromises have to be made by schools trying to implement reforms. A variety of types of school formats have evolved and were identified earlier in this chapter. The application of each of these formats to a particular setting always requires unique compromises. However, the key to planning reform is to explicitly recognize the compromises and their implications. The planning process presented throughout this book outlines the decisions that need to be made, and examples of those made by a sample of schools.

MACRO CURRICULAR DECISIONS

Even though schools may not be able to adopt all of the innovations outlined, they can and should move toward the best approximation of their ideals within their unique environments. Regardless which of the specific types of formats and innovations a particular school, school district, or state wishes to develop, the planning process is similar. The processes are similar for developing career major programs, Tech Prep, academies, or magnet schools. The major difference is in how many innovations will be expected. This will determine where the planning process stops. For example, if the instruction is to be delivered around career major contexts, then career majors must be identified. This will result in the need to identify reasonable courses relative to each career major. If the instruction is not to be integrated between different subject matter areas, then integration does not need to be planned. However, integration must be planned if it is to be implemented. If students are to be homogeneously grouped according to career interests as in a magnet school, integration is quite possible.

The Reform Strategy Checklist (Figure 2.2) presents major questions a school needs to answer as they create a vision of their reform strategy. The questions are ordered in terms of the magnitude of the change that would need to be undertaken by a typical comprehensive high school.

FIGURE 2.2 THE REFORM STRATEGY CHECKLIST

- Will instructors be responsible for showing how what they are teaching is used in the real world?

- Will instructors be required to develop exercises that students will complete to actually apply the content being taught?

- Will instructors be required to create problem scenarios that will require students to reflect on how what is being taught relates to their career interests and how it is applied?

- Will students interested in a particular career or content specialty be identified and treated as a group?

- Will separate courses be designed for members of designated groups?

- Will courses designed for a specific group be integrated, requiring instructors of these courses to jointly plan instruction?

- Will the curricula and courses designed for a specific group be treated as separate schools within a comprehensive school, or will they be separated administratively and/or physically?

- Will students be expected to take part in planned community-based experiences?

- Will the high school curriculum be articulated with postsecondary programs, requiring joint planning between the institutions?

3

ESTABLISHING CAREER MAJORS

This chapter details how to establish career majors as organizers for a school's curriculum. It provides background information for those interested only in how it is done, and it provides a step-by-step procedure for those who wish to do it. The procedures can be used to organize one or more programs around majors. For those who wish to actual establish majors, they should complete the worksheets in at the end of this chapter as they proceed through the chapter.

WHAT ARE CAREER MAJORS?

A career major is similar to a major in college. It is a set of courses recommended for students with a particular career interest. As with a college major, there is a set of core courses to be taken by all students and a set of electives. Within the new vision of a high school, it is important not to equate the concept of a career major with only those types of programs that have historically been part of traditional vocational education. Career majors can be developed in the arts, sciences, health, engineering, etc. They are essential ingredients within academies and magnet schools in addition to Tech Prep programs. As was pointed out in the Chapter 2 examples, career majors can be developed around any envisioned career.

Although many use the terms career pathways and career majors synonymously, here they are distinguished as follows.

♦ Career pathways are students' visions of how they might individually prepare for their future lives and work; the path a student might follow to prepare for his/her perceived future.

♦ Career majors are curricular organizers that focus
   on clusters of career pathways that require common sets of competencies.

For example, individual students may be interested in a
variety of specific manufacturing careers and create visions of
the pathways of courses they should take and experiences
they should have to get there. However, from a curricular
point of view it would not be possible to have a separate high
school program to accommodate each student's vision. Therefore, a major could be designed to address the cluster of manufacturing careers which could provide content common to
most manufacturing careers. This is similar to the way majors
are developed in colleges. Students in a particular major, such
as business, later go into a variety of different jobs. However,
the courses in the major give them general preparation to enter that variety of jobs. Majors are ways of efficiently focusing
and defining curricula and courses around typical students'
visions of their futures.

As career majors are being developed, it is important to remember that they should not evolve into tracks the way the
college preparatory, vocational education, and general education programs did in the past. They must be designed so students have the same flexibility in changing majors as is available to college students. This means that all majors should
contain at least the same minimal set of rigorous academic
courses in addition to career courses related to a particular career focus. This is equivalent to the liberal education requirements in college that all students must meet regardless of their
professional interests. This common set of courses allows college students to more efficiently change majors by taking a
new set of professional courses, but they have a common core
of liberal education courses.

In thinking about majors, it is also important to redefine
what are considered to be the career courses associated with a
career major. If all students will be encouraged to declare a career major, courses designated as career courses must go beyond the typical vocational education courses of the past. To
accomplish this, the past distinctions between vocational
courses and academic courses no longer make sense. Some

courses with traditional academic labels might be part of the common core of liberal education courses required of everyone, and some might only be required for selected career majors. Those academic courses required for a specific career major, which go beyond the common core of basic academic courses, are really career courses. For example, at the San Diego High School Writing Academy there are general writing courses that support the curriculum across the entire school. There are also writing classes in journalism, writing workshops, and writing experience courses that are courses designed for students who have selected writing as their potential career. Under the old way of thinking about courses, these students would have been only taking academic courses and no career courses because language arts was academic and writing was not a vocational course. This example demonstrates why thinking about courses as academic and vocational no longer makes sense. Writing courses focused on preparing writers are just as much career courses as past vocational welding courses. As career majors are developed, it is more meaningful to think about majors in terms of a common core of general academic preparation plus a set of career courses, than to think of the courses as academic versus career courses.

DEFINING THE ROLE OF MAJORS IN THE SCHOOL

The first step in developing career majors within a high school is to clarify the overall view of how majors will fit into the curriculum structure and philosophy of the school. This requires policy decisions at the highest level. These decisions ultimately have to be made by the school board with input from the administration, teachers, parents, and students. Two sets of major decisions need to be made. One regarding which students will be expected to participate in career majors, and one regarding the expectations for courses within a major. Once these decisions are available, they provide parameters for the type of reform to take place.

First, which students will be expected to participate in majors?

- ◆ Will all students in the school be expected to define a career major that will become the focal point for the courses they take?
- ◆ Will only those students who are not planning on attending four-year colleges and universities be asked to define a major?
- ◆ Will only those students who plan on taking part in a traditional career program be expected to define a major?

Second, what expectations will there be for instructors of courses to be included in career majors?

- ◆ Will majors be viewed as combinations of existing courses taught in the same way as they have been taught in the past?
- ◆ Will courses be expected to change in order to reflect the applied contexts of the majors?
- ◆ Will courses within a major need to be integrated?
- ◆ Will courses be expected to include community-based experiences?

Programs which elect to go only as far as using combinations of existing courses to create career majors are called "career major programs," as defined in Chapter 2. This practice is analogous to using college courses that are included in many majors but are taught focused on disciplines. Figures 3.1 through 3.4 (pp. 59–62) present such sample career major programs of study, with minor editing, for four different majors at St. Francis High School in St. Francis, Minnesota. Notice that they all have a common academic core of rigorous academic courses. Each also has a group of career elective courses, which is recommended for the particular major focus. The common academic core facilitates students changing career majors as they progress through high school by just choosing a different set of coherent career major courses. Changing career

(Text continues on page 63.)

FIGURE 3.1 BUSINESS, MANAGERIAL, AND SALES MAJOR

	Grade 9	Grade 10	Grade 11	Grade 12
Required Classes (Academic Core)	English 9 Civics (S) Physical Science Applied Math I, Algebra, or Geometry Physical Education 9 Futures Prep (1 Qtr)	English 10 American History Biology Health(S) Physical Education 10 Applied Math II, Alg. I, Geometry, or Alg. II	English 11 Social Problems Geography (S)	English 12 Social Studies Choices: Applied Economics (S) Current Affairs (S)
Career Core Electives	Intro. to Business (S)	Intro. to Business (S)	Computer Applications Accounting I/II Business Methods, Comm. & Tech. (S) Store Operations Small Business Mgmt. (S)	Computer Applications I/II Business Law (S) Integrated Business Simulation Principles of Marketing

(S) Semester Length

Figure 3.2 Artistic, Musical, and Literary Major

	Grade 9	Grade 10	Grade 11	Grade 12
Required Classes (Academic Core)	English 9 Civics (S) Physical Science Applied Math I, Algebra, or Geometry Physical Education 9 Futures Prep (1 Qtr)	English 10 American History Biology Health(S) Physical Education 10 Applied Math II, Alg. I, Geometry, or Alg. II	English 11 Social Problems Geography (S)	English 12 Social Studies Choice
Career Core Electives	Drawing I/II (S) Basic Graphic Arts (S) Basic Photography (S) Choir Band	Drawing I/II (S) Individualized Art (S) Painting (S) Sculpture (S) Architectural Design I/II Basic/Adv. Graphic Arts (S) Basic/Adv. Photog. (S) Choir Band Interior Design	Drawing I/II (S) Individualized Art (S) Painting (S) Sculpture (S) Architectural Design I/II Basic/Adv. Graphic Arts (S) Basic/Adv. Photog. (S) Choir Band Interior Design	Drawing I/II (S) Individualized Art (S) Painting (S) Sculpture (S) Architectural Design I/II Basic/Adv. Graphic Arts (S) Basic/Adv. Photog. (S) Choir Band Interior Design

(S) Semester Length

FIGURE 3.3 SKILLED TRADES AND TECHNICAL MAJOR

	Grade 9	Grade 10	Grade 11	Grade 12
Required Classes (Academic Core)	English 9 Civics (S) Physical Science Applied Math I, Algebra, or Geometry Physical Education 9 Futures Prep (1 Qtr)	English 10 American History Biology Health(S) Physical Education 10 Applied Math II, Alg. I, Geometry, or Alg. II	English 11 Social Problems Geography (S)	English 12 Social Studies Choices: Applied Economics (S) Current Affairs (S)
Career Core Electives	Wood Technology Basic Drafting Metal Technology (S) Power Mechanic (S)	Computer Apps. I Keyboarding I (S) Wood Technology (S) Basic Drafting (S) Metal Technology Power Mechanics (S)	Chemistry Principles of Technology I Architectural Design I (S) Auto Mechanics I (S) Applied Electricity (S) Electrical Power and Wiring (S) Computer Apps. II (S) Hot Metals (S)	Architectural Design II Construction Trades Auto Mechanics II Machine Drawing (S) Digital Electronics I/II Electronics Occupations Vocational Machine Shop Diesel Engines Vocational Welding

(S) Semester Length

FIGURE 3.4 SCIENTIFIC AND TECHNOLOGY MAJOR

	Grade 9	Grade 10	Grade 11	Grade 12
Required Classes (Academic Core)	English 9 Civics (S) Physical Science Applied Math I, Algebra, or Geometry Physical Education 9 Futures Prep (1 Qtr)	English 10 American History Biology Health(S) Physical Education 10 Applied Math II, Alg. I, Geometry, or Alg. II	English 11 Social Problems Geography (S)	English 12 Social Studies Choices: Psychology Social Psychology (S) Current Affairs (S)
Career Core Electives	Keyboarding I (S)	Computer Apps. I (S) Keyboarding I (S) Exploring Health Occupations (S)	Applied Math III, Alg. I, Geometry, or Alg. II Applied Electricity Digital Electronics I/II Machine Drawing (S) Chemistry	Trigonometry (S) Principles of Technology I/Physics Electronics Occupations Computer Apps. II (S) Machine Shop I (S) Basic Computer (S) Medical Terminology (S) Anatomy and Physiology (S)

(S) Semester Length

majors part way through high school will obviously affect the depth of the immersion into a career area students might achieve because they will not have as much time to pursue the major as those who selected it earlier. However, given the objectives of the new high school career programs, this is not viewed as a serious problem. Students are not expected to exit the major ready for direct employment in skilled, technical, or professional occupations. The purpose of the major is to serve as an anchor for learning and the development of basic technical skills and knowledge within a career area consistent with the student's vision of his/her future. The motivational value of a career major, the ability to anchor education to visions of the future, and the development of at least some basic skills and knowledge considered to be core within a career area will have been achieved even if students change majors.

What they will be lacking are some of the core career competencies. Although this may restrict their ability to enter postsecondary programs at an advanced level, they will be able to make up the deficits later. This will also be true for career specific academic courses.

Also, notice that the course electives include additional career academic courses that go beyond the general academic core for some career majors, as well as other career courses. For example, chemistry and trigonometry are career course electives in the scientific and technology major. Therefore, within the context of planning career majors, advanced academic courses recommended for a career major as well as more specifically occupationally focused career courses are included in the recommended career electives.

As students select elective courses it is important that they select a reasonable number of occupationally focused career courses that address actually practice in the career area. This is important because the occupational career courses provide the contextual background for significant creative problem solving. It is not appropriate for a student to select only the academic courses as part of the electives and none of the occupational career courses. The value of the context of the career major as a focal point for instruction gets lost. In some cases, it may be advisable to actually specify a required set of core career courses.

The Major Course Selection Worksheet is presented as Figure 3.12 (p. 73). It provides a format for the development of career majors. But first, a school must identify the career majors to be developed.

DETERMINING A SCHOOL'S MAJORS

Given that the questions listed at the beginning of this chapter have been addressed and the decision has been made to organize all or part of the curriculum around career majors, the next step is to identify the career majors that will be available within the school. During the selection of the career majors, two important criteria must be considered.

♦ Majors must be consistent with student visions if they are to be of educational value.

♦ Majors can be defined only as narrowly as local curriculum resources permit.

It is important to remember the purposes of the career majors presented earlier. Career majors should not only be curriculum organizers, but they are intended to motivate and provide a context for students to develop critical problem solving skills in preparation for the knowledge/imagination age. Therefore, majors cannot be developed solely on what educators believe the career foci of the students should be. Majors must also be developed around the actual career aspirations of the students. Organizing the curriculum around career majors and then assigning students to career areas that do not reflect their aspirations will not allow the educational power of career majors to be realized. For a career major to truly influence a student's learning, the student must see the content and the experiences as being highly relevant to her/his future.

Therefore, it is recommended that a school getting ready to adopt career majors survey the students and ask them what they currently think are their career aspirations. Typically, their aspirations will cluster around the types of career majors listed in Figure 3.5. This sample list was compiled from actual school catalogues.

Figure 3.5 Sample Career Majors

- Arts and literature
- Skilled and Technical
- Science and technology
- Business and management
- Family and consumer science
- Agriculture and Environment
- Construction
- Legal and government
- Manufacturing

However, within each community and geographic area there are unique career aspirations based on the local economy and other social factors. What typically results from such a survey is a validation of some of the more common career majors and the uncovering of other career majors that might be appropriate for sizable portions of the local student body. It is important not to confuse the idea of addressing local career aspirations with the notion of addressing the local economic needs of the community. Although these two notions do not necessarily have to be in opposition, the key is that the majors reflect student aspirations. If they also address local economic development that should be a possible side effect and not the central focus.

During the identification of the career majors, parents and the community should also be involved. Involving these groups is not only important in determining which majors there should be, but it is also important in eliciting their future support which will be critical for the later implementation of the career majors. Parents need to be aware of why career majors are being developed so fears can be eliminated and participation can be obtained. Business and industry, and other community groups need to be involved because they can add realism to choices and will most likely be called upon later to provide community-based experiences.

After clarifying which career majors might provide the foci for student learning, it is also important to determine the extent to which the school can actually provide the curriculum to support each career major. Because larger schools, technical high schools, academies, and magnet schools tend to have separate facilities and large student bodies with the same career interests, they can often justify developing specialized courses and hiring specialized staff. For example, a technical high school might be able to support a construction trades major because it has the facilities and staff to offer the specialized courses required (see Figure 3.6). Such a major would include major courses requiring specialized faculty and equipment.

FIGURE 3.6 CONSTRUCTION MAJOR COURSES

- ◆ Highly focused
  - Architectural drafting
  - Welding
  - Electrical power and wiring
  - Site preparation
  - Construction financing
  - Masonry
  - Plumbing

Most smaller schools would not have the ability to deliver a curriculum composed of such specialized courses. Therefore, they might need to offer courses that are more general and majors applicable to a larger range of careers. Figure 3.7 presents a skilled and technical major, which would include construction, plus other technical occupations. Notice the more general career courses. Smaller schools may find that such broadly defined majors are the only ones they can provide given the resources available.

FIGURE 3.7 SKILLED AND
TECHNICAL MAJOR COURSE

♦ More general focus
  - Wood technology
  - Basic drafting
  - Metal technology
  - Power Mechanics
  - Machine drawing
  - Building construction
  - Architectural drafting
  - Auto mechanics
  - Electrical power
  - Welding

A good test of whether a school can realistically offer a particular major is to complete the Major Course Selection Worksheet (Figure 3.12, p. 73). The worksheet contains spaces to enter the common academic core, the career core courses, and electives including both the academic and career courses. It also allows space to enter the careers included within the career scope of the major. If the courses that can be made available in the school can not realistically support the depth of a particular major, it may be necessary to increase the breadth of the major and reduce the specificity of the career scope. *If you are interested in identifying career majors for your school, now would be the time for you to complete School Majors Worksheet (Figure 3.10, p. 71).*

DETERMINE THE SCOPE OF EACH MAJOR

While considering the majors to be offered in a school, it is also important to clarify the career scope of each major. Which career pathways will the particular major address? This is important because it helps focus the types of career activities teachers use as focal points for their instruction, and it will help students select a major based on their visions of their career pathways. For example, the list of possible careers students might enter upon completing a Business Managerial and Sales Major is presented in Figure 3.8. Sample careers students might enter upon completing an Arts and Communication major are presented in Figure 3.9 (p. 70). Notice that the career scope of each of these majors includes careers one might prepare for by completing education at the community or technical college (one to three years) level, or the four-year college level. This is consistent with the view that majors should be developed to accommodate those preparing for skilled, technical or professional careers.

If you are interested in planning the career scope of your majors, this would be the time to complete the Scope of the Major Worksheet (Figure 3.11, p. 72) for each major. If you are interested in developing lists of courses to be included in each major, this would be the time to complete the Major Course Selection Worksheet (Figure 3.12, p. 73) for each major.

Now that we have identified the career majors that will be the curriculum organizers, their career scopes, and course combinations, this information can be used to modify the curriculum and to counsel the students. The information can also be used to inform instructors of the range of student career majors that they might need to address in their classes. This will allow instructors to use appropriate contexts when showing how what they are teaching can be applied in areas of student interest.

If the development of career major programs composed of existing courses is the only goal that the school wishes to accomplish, their curriculum revision process is complete. However, if there is a desire to modify how courses are taught, or if there is a desire to encourage integrated instruction between instructors of courses within a major, the school must move to the next step. That step is to develop and integrate the courses as described in the next chapter.

FIGURE 3.8 CAREER SCOPE OF A
BUSINESS, MANAGERIAL, AND SALES MAJOR

1–3 Years Community College/ Technical College Education	*4–Year College Education*
Typical Careers	*Typical Careers*
Administrative Assistant	Attorney
Assistant Buyer	Bank Officer
Associate Accountant	Business Teacher
Aviation Operator Specialist	City Manager
Bookkeeper	Claims Adjuster
Computer Graphic Specialist	Computer Programmer
Computer Operator	Accountant
Customer Service Rep	Dietary Manager
Fashion Merchandiser	Editorial Assistant
Flight Attendant	Economist
General Office Clerk	Financial Manager
General Secretary	General Manager/Hotel Manager
Hotel & Motel Management	Marketing Director
Income Tax Consultant	Media Director
Insurance Claims Specialist	Personnel Officer
Legal Secretary	Production Planner
Legal Assistant	Public Relations Specialist
Medical Record Technician	Real Estate Broker
Medical Secretary	Safety Inspector
Microcomputer Support and Network Administrator	Sales Manager
Office Administrator	Small Business Operator/Owner
Personnel Assistant	Stock Broker
Paralegal	Title Examiner
Postal Clerk	Urban Planner
Property Manager	Underwriter
Receptionist	Entrepreneur
Data Processing	

Mesabi East High School, Aurora, MN

Figure 3.9 Career Scope of an
Arts and Communication Major

1–3 Years Community College/ Technical College Education	*4–Year College Education*
Typical Careers	*Typical Careers*
Audio Recording Specialist	Architect
Audio Visual Media Producer	Advertising/Public Relations
Broadcast Technician	Apparel Designer
Camera Operator	Artist
Commercial Photographer	Art Historian
Computer-Aided Designer	Broadcaster (Radio & TV)
Court Reporter	Choreographer
Color or Printing Press Operator	Columnist
Electronic Publisher	Commercial Artist
Film Maker	Copy Writer
Graphic Designer/Artist	Costume Designer
Jeweler	Creative Writer
Instrument Repairer	Dancer
Lighting Technician	Editor/Education Administrator
Model/Motion Picture Technician	Film Maker
Paralegal Assistant	Foreign Language Interpreter
Printer	Industrial Design
Radio and Television Broadcaster	Illustrator
Stage Manager	Interior Designer
Technical Artist	Journalist
Travel Agent	Media Specialist
Video Production Technician	Museum Curator
Visual Artist	Musician
	Philosopher
	Photojournalist
	Publisher
	Teacher
	Technical Writer
	Theater Arts: Actor, Actress, Director
	Sculptor/Video Producer

Mesabi East High School, Aurora, MN

FIGURE 3.10 SCHOOL MAJORS WORKSHEET

School: _____

Majors: _____

1. _____

2. _____

3. _____

4. _____

5. _____

6. _____

7. _____

8. _____

9. _____

10. _____

11. _____

12. _____

13. _____

14. _____

FIGURE 3.11 SCOPE OF THE MAJOR WORKSHEET (FOR EACH MAJOR)

Major name: _____

       List a sample of specific occupations or life roles that represent the scope to be addressed within the major.

Years of Additional Education Required

		1–3	*4 or more*
1.	_____	☐	☐
2.	_____	☐	☐
3.	_____	☐	☐
4.	_____	☐	☐
5.	_____	☐	☐
6.	_____	☐	☐
7.	_____	☐	☐
8.	_____	☐	☐
9.	_____	☐	☐
10.	_____	☐	☐
11.	_____	☐	☐
12.	_____	☐	☐
13.	_____	☐	☐
14.	_____	☐	☐
15.	_____	☐	☐
16.	_____	☐	☐
17.	_____	☐	☐
18.	_____	☐	☐
19.	_____	☐	☐

FIGURE 3.12 MAJOR COURSE SELECTION WORKSHEET

Major title: _____

Type of program: _____

(Tech Prep, Academy, Magnet School)

Grade 9	Grade 10	Grade 11	Grade 12	Typical Careers
Required Academic Core	Required Academic Core	Required Academic Core	Required Academic Core	
Career Core Electives (academic and career)	Career Core Electives (academic and career)	Career Core Electives (academic and career)	Career Core Electives (academic and career)	

Use * to indicate career core courses.

4

DEVELOPING CAREER MAJOR COURSES

DETAILING COURSES TO BE DEVELOPED

Chapter 3 dealt with establishing career majors and identifying the courses to be part of career major programs, Tech Prep programs, academies, or magnet schools. If the courses within the major are to be revised or adapted, the next step is to detail and develop each course within the major. In some instances, this means creating new courses, or it may mean documenting and revising existing courses. Few existing traditional courses will contain all the elements of a good career major course.

When developing a career major course it is important to clearly specify the broad goals of the course, the expected grade levels of students and course length, the specific content to be taught, and the content from other major courses that can be reinforced. It is also important to determine the instructional strategies that will underlie the courses. In terms of this book, this means which of the innovations identified in Chapter 2 are to be implemented. If courses in a major are to be taught as they have been in the past, it is still important to clarify this information to clearly understand what they are to contribute to a major.

As indicated in earlier chapters, majors composed of combinations of existing courses traditionally taught are obviously the easiest to adopt. Developing courses around the contexts of a career major is a challenge for both academic and career instructors. There is a common myth that since career course instructors teach content around occupations, their traditional courses already meet the requirements of career major courses. That is not so. Career instructors in some fields, such as business education, have tended to teach many of their courses in much the same way that social studies courses are taught. They have taught business law, business communication, etc., with a focus on the content they are teaching and not on how the content might be applied in a broad career major. Other career instructors, such as construction instructors, have focused on specific occupations such as carpentry and not on addressing the broad scope of a career major. Many have not focused on problem solving and learning activities outside the classroom. Therefore, developing courses and teaching content in the context of career majors is a challenge for teachers in all fields.

If the courses in the major are to be taught around applied career examples, this requires traditional courses to be adjusted to show students how the content is relevant and useful. This is often difficult for academic instructors. Many have not had experiences within the various careers. They might need to look to career course instructors for help in identifying relevant examples. On the other hand, if career course instructors are going to be expected to reinforce the content of academic courses within the major, they might need help. They may or may not clearly understand the content taught in the academic courses. Therefore, the academic instructors and the career course instructors typically need to get together to discuss what each will be teaching and how that might be applied in each other's courses.

If the courses are to be truly integrated, this often requires the development of joint projects in which students can apply what is being learned in one class to actual activities in another class. For example, if the math instructor is teaching ratios and the manufacturing instructor is teaching calculating gear settings for a lathe, the math instructor could use gear settings as an applied example, and the manufacturing instructor could explicitly indicate how the application of what was being learned in math applies to manufacturing. Integration is a major premise underlying the development of majors within Tech Prep programs.

DIFFERENCES BETWEEN CAREER AND ACADEMIC CAREER MAJOR COURSE DEVELOPMENT

There are some major differences between the planning of career and academic career major courses. Career courses typically focus on providing students with a representative set of competencies and knowledge regarding how work is conducted in occupations within the scope of a career major. Courses are developed around the technology and career practices within the major. Therefore, the first step is to identify core career content relevant to the career major. The challenge is to ensure that it is focused on a sample of representative competencies and knowledge associated with the occupational scope of the major, and not a specific occupation. Once the career content is identified, the next step is to identify relevant content from other courses in the major that can be reinforced as part of a career major curriculum.

On the other hand, academic instructors usually start their course development by identifying topics to be covered from the taxonomy of the discipline. The topics are generally those that the school board has determined need to be covered within a given course. Academic textbooks usually focus on teaching the content and not applications. Therefore, if the academic instructors are going to teach in an applied manner to support the career majors of their students, they must identify an array of examples of how their content might be related to the students' majors. As was explained in Chapters 1 and 2, the size of this task increases as the diversity of the career majors of the students in their classes increases. This diversity can be determined by reviewing the potential students' career majors and the career scopes of those majors as identified in Chapter 3. Therefore, academic instructors also have a two-stage process. They first need to identify the core subject matter of their courses, and then they need to identify career major examples of the application of that content.

As indicated earlier, if the courses within the major are to be integrated, the career and academic instructors need to go an additional step. They need to identify joint student projects that will require the application of what they are learning in the various courses within the major.

During the following discussion of detailing courses, where the process differs between the career and academic courses, the differences will be highlighted. In each section, the development of the career courses as part of a career major will be presented first.

DETAILING CAREER MAJOR COURSES

The detailing of both career and academic courses will be presented in the context of planning a career major course syllabus. The author's experience in working with teachers has shown that thinking in terms of syllabus planning makes the process more concrete and meaningful to teachers. Because this particular plan is designed to be used by teachers as they are planning, it presents more detail than students would typically find meaningful and, therefore, needs to be modified before actually being presented to students. The syllabus provided to the students should conform to the format used by a particular school.

A blank copy of the format for detailing a syllabus is presented at the end of this chapter in Figure 4.9 (pp. 105–109). It contains sections around which the course development or review process should be conducted. Spaces are provided in which to enter choices when planning a course. Some sections of the detailing guide have two parts. One is for planning career courses and the other is for planning academic courses. However, most sections are the same for both types of courses. Also at the end of this chapter is Figure 4.10 (pp. 110–113), which presents a detailed sample syllabus plan for a computer applications course developed by a high school teacher.

The basic steps of the career major course planning procedure are:

+ State the course title and content description
+ Define the overall career scope of the major
+ Clarify the instructional strategy

- ◆ State the course parameters (course length, grade level(s) served, prerequisites)
- ◆ State the broad course goals
- ◆ State specific technical or academic competencies which are the central focus of the course
- ◆ State sample major career activities representative of the careers within the scope
- ◆ Identify relevant content from other career major courses that will be reinforced.
- ◆ Identify relevant community-based activities
- ◆ Plan student assessment

COURSE TITLE AND CONTENT DESCRIPTION

The first item to be entered into the syllabus plan is the title of the course being developed. The course should be one of the career major courses as identified in Chapter 3. The course title is placed in section A (see pp. 105 and 110) of the plan. In addition to indicating the course title, it is useful to develop a brief description of the course content. This helps those outside of the particular subject matter area to get a clear view of the range of the course content. For example, high school trigonometry is well understood and needs little explanation. However, if the title of the course is construction, it is important to provide a narrative description. In some cases a construction course might focus on carpentry, at other times it might be an overview course that covers basics of carpentry, masonry, electrical wiring, and so on. The sample course syllabus indicates that the course will address competencies in basic word processing and spreadsheet development in the context of preparing business documents.

OVERALL COURSE CAREER SCOPE

Developing the career scope of a major was presented in Chapter 3. The career scope refers to the types of careers and/or occupations the major will address. If the course being developed only addresses one career major, the careers used to describe the career scope of that major are placed in section B (see p. 105) of the syllabus planner. However, in some cases the course may serve students from more than one major. Therefore, the career scope of a particular course may be larger than that of any one major. For example, an economics course might serve students from a business major, and a legal and government major. In that case, the career scope of each of the majors must be addressed and entered into section B. The career scope is used later to make sure the sample applications of the course content reflect the range of situations representative of the career scopes of the majors from which the students will come. It is a good idea for all instructors who will teach courses for a career major to meet and discuss the nature of the major in order to complete this part of their syllabus plans. Representative occupations from the career scope of the sample course presented in Figure 4.10, section B (p. 110), are accountant, data processor, office administrator, business manager, and entrepreneur.

COURSE INSTRUCTIONAL STRATEGY

Section C (see p. 105) of the course syllabus planner presents a sample course instructional strategy. It should be edited or replaced by each instructor. It should fit the requirements of the particular school and course being developed. The strategy should reflect the nature of the innovations that are to be put in place as determined in Chapter 2. The way the strategy is stated often represents the particular instructor's interpretation of the direction the school is going to take. It is important to develop this section carefully because it has major implications for what others will expect from the course. The sample syllabus plan in Figure 4.10, section C (p. 110) shows how one instructor modified the statement.

COURSE PARAMETERS

The course parameters define constraints within which the course must be developed. They include the length of the course, the grade levels of the students who will be expected to come to the course, and any prerequisites that might be expected of the students. It is important for an instructor to clarify these parameters early. They provide a basis for answering questions such as: (a) How much time will I have to teach the course and how much content can I reasonably expect to cover within that time? (b) What grade level students will be in the course and how will this affect what I think they will bring to the course in terms of experience, other courses taken, and maturity? and (c) Where can I begin with the presentation of the content of the course? A definition of these basic parameters should be entered in section D (see p. 106) of the syllabus planner. For the sample course in Figure 4.10 (p. 111), the decision was made to offer it for one semester to students in grades 10 through 12 who have completed an introduction to business course.

BROAD COURSE GOALS

The broad course goals indicate what the course is expected to accomplish. This is an area that at first seems to be easy; it seems easy because many instructors first think in terms of getting students to master their content. This is a reflection of the past discipline-based orientation. Certainly, first and foremost, each course should adequately present its core content, which is the subject matter focus of the course. Therefore, students should be expected to master the academic and/or technical content of the course. However, in addition to accomplishing this goal, most courses are now expected to accomplish or assist with the accomplishment of other goals. Some of those goals directly reflect the changing educational philosophy discussed earlier and others reflect general societal expectations of all of education, or local and state expectations. Some of the broad goals, in addition to mastering the content that instructors have provided, are:

- ◆ All students will apply the course content to their career and life visions.
- ◆ Students will see how the content taught relates to their lives and work.
- ◆ Content from other courses will be reinforced to show relevance.

- Students will participate in community-based experiences related to their majors.

- Students will experience authentic career activities representative of the career major(s).

- Students will complete work to workplace quality standards.

- Students will adopt safe practices and safety consciousness.

- Students will solve workplace problems during the completion of projects.

- Students will research a career of personal interest to which course content applies.

Often those developing career majors also embrace the general employability goals established by the Secretary's Commission on Necessary Employment Competencies (SCANS). They were discussed in Chapter 1 but are presented here again for ready reference. They provide a set of competencies thought to be important regardless of the career a person enters. Those competencies are:

Three-Part Foundation

- *Basic competencies:* Reads, writes, performs arithmetic and mathematical operations, listens, and speaks.

- *Thinking competencies:* Thinks creatively, makes decisions, solves problems, visualizes, knows how to learn, and reasons.

- *Personal qualities:* Displays responsibility, self-esteem, sociability, self-management, and integrity and honesty.

SCANS Five Competencies

- *Resources:* Identifies, organizes, plans and allocates resources.

- *Interpersonal:* Works with others.

- *Information:* Acquires and uses information.

- *Systems:* Understands complex inter-relationships.
- *Technology:* Works with a variety of technologies.

When selecting broad course goals, care should be taken because the goals selected represent a commitment on the part of the instructor to include learning activities in the course directed at each goal. In other words, it is not enough to just list the goals as things that would be nice to accomplish. After the course is totally developed, it is not unreasonable for people reviewing the syllabus plan to ask, "Please indicate the learning activities in the course that will be directed at accomplishing each goal."

The actual delivery of instruction on the broad goals, other than teaching the core content of the course, should not be thought of as being in competition with the teaching of the core content. The accomplishment of the other broad goals should take place during the teaching of the core content. This is done by changing the teaching methodology surrounding the teaching of core content. For example, if the instructor adopted the goal of helping students learn to work with others, group assignments could be given for some portions of the course rather than individual assignments. If the instructor adopted the goal of developing problem solving ability, the instructor could assign students to apply what is being taught to situations from their career areas and to report back to the class. This is in contrast to stopping the teaching of the core content (e.g., language arts, power and electricity) and delivering an entire unit on team building or problem solving with exercises not directly related to the course's core content.

The lists of broad course goals presented above by no means represent an exhaustive list. Each person designing a course to be part of a career major must list those goals that the designer would like the course to achieve. Those goals should be listed in section E of the syllabus planner in Figure 4.9 (see p. 106). The broad goals selected by the instructor for the sample syllabus in Figure 4.10 (see p. 111) are that upon completion of this course students will:

- Master relevant technical competencies
- Manage business resources

- ◆ Become a productive group participant
- ◆ Become a purposeful thinker
- ◆ Identify a career pathway and develop and maintain lifework plan
- ◆ Research a career of personal interest
- ◆ Become a self-directed learner
- ◆ Plan and organize resources
- ◆ Interpret and communicate information
- ◆ Select technology to complete tasks

SPECIFIC TECHNICAL OR ACADEMIC COMPETENCIES

Each course, whether it is considered to be an academic or a career course, has a central content focus. An algebra course focuses on algebra; a microcomputer course focuses on operating microcomputers, and a carpentry course on carpentry. When students complete each of these courses they should have been taught the important content related to each central focus. This is an important concept because some people think that the content students should learn is the academic content and that career courses are merely vehicles for reinforcing that content through applied applications. That view is not consistent with developing career majors with the intent of students becoming oriented to careers of their choice and developing a sufficient command of competencies required within those careers to support creative problem solving and future preparation for their careers. Career courses cannot be developed around episodic content just as academic courses cannot. Just as an algebra course should include certain content to ensure students have a command of the important algebra competencies, career courses must also include certain content to ensure students have command of the important content related to the career major. Both need to be well planned to ensure that students are developing important competencies.

Once the central content of a course is determined, that content will probably need to be taught differently in the context of a career major than it was traditionally taught in the past. Academic content cannot be taught abstractly with the focus totally on the discipline. Career courses cannot be taught solely as a set of procedural techniques required within an occupation. The academic courses need to be taught around meaningful applications within the career majors served by the courses. The career courses need to be taught in a manner that supports what is being learned in the career major academic courses and need to present the knowledge base that supports meaningful application of career skills. In addition, each of the courses needs to be oriented toward eventually enabling students to solve creative problems in their career majors.

Therefore, during the development of each course, the basic core content to be taught should be clearly identified and all students completing the course should be expected to master those competencies. In addition to completing the core competencies, students should be expected to plan and complete other optional learning activities focused on their individual career interests with the career major. For example, if the career major is manufacturing, some students might be interested in becoming a welder and some a mechanical engineer. Therefore, some students will complete some of their assignments in terms of welding and some in terms of mechanical engineering. The culminating activity regarding all competencies taught, core or optional within a course, should require students to creatively apply the content to situations within their career visions.

As indicated earlier, the identification of the actual content to be taught in a career major course is one of the sections where academic and career course planning procedures tend to vary. Identification of the core competencies to be addressed within career courses is typically accomplished by identifying occupational competencies common within occupations included within the career scope of the major. The competencies can be identified by first obtaining occupational analyses of each of the careers within the scope of the major. Such analyses are readily available from a number of curriculum centers such as the Southeastern Instructional Materials Center (www.votech-resources.com), which provides vocational curriculum and instructional resources. In addition, such information is available at the national level for selected occupations in the form of National Skill Standards (www.nssb.org), and through the Occupational Information Network (O*NET) (www.doleta.gov/programs/onet).

CAREER COURSE CONTENT

The occupational analyses for those occupations within the career scope identified earlier should be placed next to one another in a table such as that shown Figure 4.1. The various analyses should be examined to identify common competencies required across the occupations to be addressed within the career major. Those common competencies should be the central focus of career courses that are part of the major. When developing a specific course (e.g., computer applications), the common competencies that are associated with that course should be the focus of that course. If it is considered important to address some specific competencies associated with particular occupations within the career scope, the instructor should try to vary the occupations from which specific competencies come throughout the course. For example, in the sample table, it would not be appropriate to have all of the specific occupational competencies focused on an office administrator.

FIGURE 4.1 IDENTIFYING COMMON CAREER COMPETENCIES—BUSINESS MAJOR

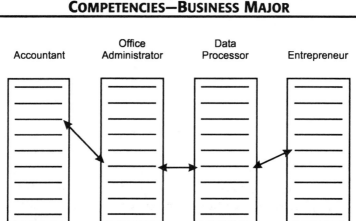

The career competencies to be taught should be stated in the form of behavioral/performance objectives. Figure 4.2 provides the suggested format for these objectives. The objectives clearly state what students are expected to be able to do in relation to the careers within the career scope. Each objective should include the verb indicating what the student will be expected to be able to do and what she/he will be expected to do it with. The examples are from the sample syllabus in Figure 4.10 (p. 111). Notice that the objectives contain performances that include what people will be expected to physically manipulate (psychomotor objectives), decisions or manipulations of information (cognitive objectives), and how they will treat things (affective objectives). It is important to not only focus on tasks requiring the physical manipulation of things.

FIGURE 4.2 SAMPLE CAREER PERFORMANCE OBJECTIVES

Verb–action	Object–what
Type	minimum of 25 words per minute
Assemble	materials for business reports
Operate	a photocopy machine
Create	a business correspondence letter
Design	a spreadsheet
Create	a spreadsheet
Synthesize	information for a business report
Treat	coworkers with respect
Treat	equipment with care

ACADEMIC COURSE CONTENT

When identifying content for a typical academic course in the major, instructors often turn to well-accepted textbooks and school board and/or state approved standards. There are also national curriculum centers in each of the academic fields that provide curricular information such as the Center for Science, Mathematics and Technology Education (www.csmate. colostate.edu). As indicated earlier, the content required is often stated in terms of lists of topics or lists of performance objectives focused on in-class activities as contrasted with career activities, for example, quadratic equations, or list three types of poems. Within the context of career majors, the core content focus of the academic courses should remain the same and people taking a particular academic course within the context of any career major should be held to the same standards as all other students taking that course. The difference is that the content within career major courses should be taught in the context of the career majors. For example, if algebra is to be part of the basic academic core for all students in the school, students in a manufacturing, business, arts and literary, or science major would be expected to master the same core elements of algebra. However, teachers should be expected to show applications of the content to career activities from the majors and students in each major should be required to apply the content in the context of their individual majors.

Therefore, it is preferable that when academic courses are part of a career major, that the content be stated as a set of behavioral objectives focused on applications to careers. To accomplish this, academic instructors should go through a two-stage procedure to turn topics into behavioral learning objectives to support career majors. The first stage is to re-state topics as performance objectives phrased in terms of what students should be able to do with the content after leaving the course. For example, if the topic of "temperature" is being taught to students in a health major so that they learn to determine a person's temperature, then that content should be taught around taking a person's temperature. All of the content typically taught about temperature as a topic could still be taught, but students would understand how this knowledge would be useful in taking a temperature. Figure 4.3 presents a list of topics from a variety of academic courses and the same content stated in terms of performance objectives. The important distinction between topics and performance objectives is that the performance objectives indicate what the student is expected to do after instruction is complete.

FIGURE 4.3 CONVERTING ACADEMIC TOPICS TO PERFORMANCE OBJECTIVES

	Performance Objectives	
Topics	*Verb*	*Object-Content*
1. Quadratic equations	1. Solve	quadratic equations
2. Temperature	2. Take	a temperature
3. Measurement	3. Measure	an object
4. Environmental factors	4. Identify	environmental factors

Figure 4.4 takes those general behavioral objectives and states them as career performance objectives within the context of a career major served by the course. The piece that is added is applications taken from career majors. This facilitates teaching the content in the context of the career majors served by the course.

FIGURE 4.4 ACADEMIC CAREER PERFORMANCE OBJECTIVES

Verb	*Object-Content*	*Career Major Applications*
1. Solve	Quadratic equations	To calculate gear ratios
2. Take	The temperature	Of a person
3. Measure	A machine part	In decimals
4. Measure	Windows	In fractions of an inch
5. Identify	Environmental factors	When using automotive paints

The conversion of topics to career performance objectives may require collaboration between the academic and career instructors. For example, if a math course is to be part of a manufacturing major and a construction major, the math instructor should meet with the manufacturing instructor and the construction instructor to determine career applications of the math course content within each career area. This would inform the math instructor of the types of career applications that could be used in the instructor's course, and it would inform the manufacturing and construction instructors of the type of math they should reinforce when teaching the associated career competencies. In other words, the sharing of information is very useful to both the academic and career course instructors.

In summary, the process of identifying and stating the central content for an academic course that is part of a career major often takes place in three distinct stages. First, the topics to be covered in the course are stated. Second, those topics are converted to behavioral objectives. Third, those objectives are restated as career performance objectives with the addition of career applications from the major(s) to be served by the course. If a course is to serve a number of different majors (e.g., manufacturing and construction), then the performance statements must reflect the range of the occupations in the majors. This may mean that the same performance objective may need to be stated a number of times, but each time with a different career application. For example, most measurements in manufacturing are in decimals and most in carpentry are in fractions of an inch. Therefore, some examples may need to use decimals and others fractions of an inch.

Figure 4.9, Section F (p. 107) of the syllabus planning form presents space to enter the central content of the course in the form of contextual career performance objectives consistent with a career major. It is recommended that as many as 20 objectives be stated for each course. This facilitates clear communication among instructors if they attempt to integrate instruction across courses in the major. Stating a small number of objectives typically results in very global objectives that are not precise enough to communicate well between instructors from different subject matter areas.

CAREER ACTIVITIES

As one develops courses within a career major, the teaching of the separate competencies associated with each performance objective should be anchored within authentic career activities representative of the scope of the major. Often in the past, competencies or performance objectives were taught as separate entities assuming that students would be able to apply that competency in various combinations as situations arose in life and work. In other words, if students were provided instruction on individual competencies and performance capability was verified, the teaching responsibility was met. Within the context of a career major, that approach is not recommended. Students should clearly see how individual competencies are used in combinations to address common authentic workplace activities. Meaningful work rarely requires only one competency. It usually requires combinations of competencies. Therefore, if students are to learn and problem solve within the context of a career major, they should be taught within authentic career activities representative of that major.

Career activities are units of work a supervisor would ask a person to complete on the job (job assignments). They are often thought of as major projects one would be asked to complete on the job. They also become the basis for projects students could complete in their courses.

Career activities should:

♦ Be large enough to require the performance of multiple competencies;

♦ Call for planning of multiple sub-activities in order to be completed;

♦ Call for complex intellectually challenging problem solving;

♦ Result in a real unit of work being completed.

Some sample career activities for a variety of career majors are presented in Figure 4.5. Notice that all of them require the performance of multiple competencies. Some of the specific competencies associated with some of these career activities are presented in Figure 4.6.

Figure 4.5 Sample Career Activities

Construction major
- Develop a floor plan
- Prepare cost estimates
- Build a staircase
- Build a wall
- Survey the building site

Health occupations major
- Take vital signs
- Interpret medical charts
- Decide treatment to administer
- Administer intravenous (IV)

Business major
- Write a financial report
- Evaluate alternative business opportunities
- Set up a bank account
- Layout a business office

Childcare major
- Recognize childhood illnesses
- Communicate with the medical system
- Respond to accidents

The career activities associated with a career major are typically identified by the career instructors and that information is provided to the instructors of academic courses within the major as part of the discussion of the career performance objectives presented earlier. The career activities presented in the sample syllabus plan in Figure 4.10, section G (p. 112), are prepare business correspondence, communicate orally, manage company data and records, and prepare business reports.

FIGURE 4.6 SAMPLE TECHNICAL COMPETENCIES ASSOCIATED WITH CAREER ACTIVITIES

Construction Major

Major career activity:
Build a wall

Specific technical competencies:
- Cut studs
- Create a window opening
- Calculate the number of studs
- Decide where to place windows
- Cooperate with co-workers
- Accommodate the owner

Health Occupations Major

Major career activity:
Administer intravenous (IV)

Specific technical competencies:
- Assemble equipment
- Install IV system
- Choose IV system
- Calculate IV timing
- Cooperate with nursing staff
- Treat patient with care

Business Major

Major career activity:
Write a financial report

Specific technical competencies:
- Assemble materials
- Duplicate the report
- Evaluate financial records
- Synthesize financial information
- Write in an objective tone
- Cooperate with co-workers

Childcare Major

Major career activity:
Recognize childhood illness

Specific technical competencies:
- Take child's temperature
- Check child's lymph nodes
- Consult child illness references
- Recognize symptoms of illnesses
- Maintain a calm attitude
- Comfort the child

PLANNING TO REINFORCE CONTENT
TAUGHT IN OTHER MAJOR COURSES

Although the primary purpose of each course is to ensure students master core content, an additional purpose of a career major course is to reinforce and show how content from other major courses is related. If the academic course objectives are developed as indicated above to reflect career applications, the relationship between the content of those courses and the career courses will occur naturally. It occurs because the objectives will be stated in terms of career applications. If the career instructors record the types of academic content that the academic instructors will be applying, they will know which academic content to reinforce.

However, the application of content between academic courses will not occur naturally. It is just as important to know how a math course can reinforce a language arts course in the major as it is to know how those courses reinforce career courses. The application of content between all courses within a major must be planned. If the curriculum is to be integrated around a major, this is critical. Also, it is critical if one is planning integrated instruction within a Tech Prep program. Even if the goal is not to create a totally integrated curriculum, the information is still critical in order to develop an applied curriculum.

If the procedures above have been completed, then at this point in the course development process, academic instructors will have identified their core content and the career contexts within which that content should be taught. Career instructors will also have identified their core content and the academic competencies that they should reinforce.

Notice that the word "reinforce" has been used repeatedly. One needs to make a clear distinction between assuming the responsibility for teaching a body of content and reinforcing it. A key misconception in thinking about an integrated curriculum is that each instructor becomes responsible for teaching all of the content in the major. That is not so. Instructors are responsible for teaching their core content and reinforcing content taught by other instructors. The reinforcement should take place during the teaching of their core content. For example, if a machine shop instructor asks students to write a report, that instructor should not feel the need to provide a series of lessons on writing. In an integrated curriculum, that would be the responsibility of language arts and the machine shop instructor should know enough about writing a good report so those skills can be reinforced.

The types of content from other courses in the major that might be relevant to teaching a given course and which might be reinforced can be identified by asking the questions presented in Figure 4.7.

FIGURE 4.7 IDENTIFYING RELEVANT CONTENT FROM OTHER CAREER MAJOR COURSES

- What types of *mathematics* ideas, procedures, and methods of inquiry will be required? (e.g., adding decimal numbers, 3 place addition, bisecting an angle)

- What types of *language arts* ideas, procedures, and methods of inquiry are required? (e.g., document activities, report orally, research technical specifications)

- What types of *science* ideas, procedures, and methods of inquiry will be required? (e.g., chemical reaction, leverage, mixtures)

- What types of *social studies* ideas, procedures, and methods of inquiry are required? (e.g., impact on the environment, government regulations, and interpretations by different cultures)

- What types of *career knowledge and skills* will be required or can be used as examples of applications of what is being taught? (This question would have already been answered in developing the career performance objectives described earlier.)

It is important that as one answers these questions that they be answered in terms of specific content. For example, information related to language arts content that might be reinforced should not be stated as "language arts skills." That is too global and does not give adequate direction. It should be stated in terms of specifics such as "orally communicate with co-workers" or "write a memo." In math, it might be possible to get even more specific. Rather than stating, "calculate a balance sheet," one could indicate "add and subtract." The more specificity that is possible, the more clearly focused the reinforcement and the communication with other instructors. Information gained from answering these questions can be captured in section H (p. 108) of the syllabus planning form in Figure 4.9. The sample syllabus presented in Figure 4.10 (p. 112) presents samples of the choices made by the person developing the microcomputer course.

COMMUNITY-BASED ACTIVITIES

An important dimension of the vision of the New American High School is that students have an opportunity to participate in planned community-based experiences that support their learning. Therefore, the next section of syllabus planning deals with the identification of relevant community-based activities that will help accomplish specific course goals. For example, students might be expected to explore career options as a broad course goal. To reach this goal they could be asked to visit a companies or agencies related to their career majors, interview people regarding their impressions of those careers, and list career options with their pros and cons.

At this point in the planning process, the types of community-based activities that might be used to accomplish specific course goals should be identified. In Chapter 6, details on implementing community-based experiences will be presented.

The first step in deciding how community-based activities might be included in a course is to determine which learning goals could be facilitated through community-based activities. Such activities should not be included unless they can be directly related to specific learning goals of the course. Once an appropriate goal is identified, instructors must clearly specify the purpose of the experience; for example, is it to observe and report on observations, is it to obtain information and to report on something specific, or is it to participate in actual work to develop specific skills? Once it is determined that a community-based experience might be relevant and its purpose identified, the appropriate type must be selected. Guidance in selecting among types of community-based experiences is presented in Chapter 6.

The identification of relevant community-based experience can be accomplished most easily by referring to the course objectives developed earlier in Figures 4.4 (p. 91), 4.5 (p. 94), and 4.6 (p. 95), and section F (p. 107) of the syllabus. A chart indicating the objectives to be attained and the types of community-based experiences that would be helpful should be developed. This can be done by either restating the objective and the community-based learning experience, or by placing a reference code next to the learning objective. Samples of community-based experiences and the objectives to which they relate are presented in Figure 4.10, section I (p. 113) of the sample syllabus.

STUDENT ASSESSMENT

The final section of the syllabus planning process is to specify how student learning and performance will be assessed. Student assessment around career majors is somewhat different from typical classroom evaluation. Besides determining whether students learned the core content, the focus should be on whether students can apply what they have learned to real career activities and their own career visions. An assessment plan should have three components:

1. A list of things that will be evaluated.
2. A statement of how each thing will be evaluated.
3. A statement of how the evaluations of the individual things will be assembled into a report of student progress (e.g., grading).

The assessment should focus on determining whether students:

- Are capable of applying competencies using acceptable processes.
- Can complete projects which integrate what they have learned.
- Have comprehended the information they are expected to retain.
- Can explain how associated ideas and concepts relate to their activities.
- Can behave appropriately.

Common evaluation methods include checklists, written and oral tests, and portfolio evaluations. Checklists are typically used to assess a student's ability to carry out processes. The processes can be evaluated by either observing the student perform the process (e.g., baking a cake, delivering an oral report) or by looking at the product of the process (the finished cake, math calculations). Checklists can be used to assess specific competencies and/or the completed projects. Written and oral tests are typically used to assess a student's ability to recall and meaningfully apply information. Most educators are familiar with checklists that list the items that students are to perform and/or complete, and the criteria used in judging if they have been done to expectations. They are also familiar with written and oral testing. Therefore, they will not be discussed again here.

However, the use of portfolio evaluations is relatively new and will be presented briefly. Within the context of programs organized around career majors, portfolio evaluations allow for the assessment of things beyond the mastery of the basic content of courses. Portfolios are typically used to reflect a synthesis of what a student has learned and accomplished over a period of time. Some portfolios contain collections of materials that reflect what a student has done. Such materials include reports on out of school activities, photographs of larger projects, copies of materials produced when completing projects (if they are small enough), evaluations of knowledge and performance, or any other materials that could be reviewed to judge the holistic completion of course or career major goals. If the curriculum is integrated, the portfolio could include examples of the application of content from many courses. The actual evaluation of such a portfolio can be done in a number of ways. The simplest is to check off each of the assignments to make sure they have all been completed to the performance standard established. This could be done as each assignment is completed throughout the course(s) and/or at the end when all assignments are assembled.

Thinking of portfolios as collections of materials is the most common way of thinking about them. However, it does not capture the total potential of a portfolio evaluation. The true potential is realized when students are asked to go beyond the collection of materials to reflecting on what they learned, around a set of carefully thought out questions that focus their reflection. For example, students should be expected to be able to explain what they did and why, either orally or in writing. They should also be able to explain the interrelationships among the things they learned. For a person to be truly competent, that person should be able to perform and be able to explain what they did and why. This ensures that students are not just rotely learning and that they can see relationships between what they have done.

If the curriculum is truly integrated and major projects are jointly planned and instructed by instructors from the various subject matter areas, it is possible to have the portfolio evaluation include a meeting with all instructors where the student is asked questions about what they learned. An alternative is for students to write an integrating report around a well-planned set of questions. Figure 4.8 presents a relatively simple example of an assignment given to students as a basis for a portfolio evaluation presentation. It was used to cause reflection around a career activity involving multiple subject matter areas. This type of evaluation allows for judging how individual students applied what they learned to the completion of career activities relevant to their visions of their future, and whether they understood what they applied.

FIGURE 4.8 SAMPLE PORTFOLIO ASSIGNMENT

For each career activity completed in this course, do the following:

♦ Maintain a daily log of what you did toward the completion of the project.

♦ Assemble copies of all products, tests, evaluation forms, and writing assignments. (If the product is large, ask the instructor to take a picture of it for your portfolio.)

♦ Answer each of the following questions, while reflecting on what you learned:

- Select three of the technical competencies you learned and explain why each was important in completing the project. Select one and indicate what would happen if it was left out?

- What piece of technical knowledge that you learned do you think was the most critical to the completion of the project? Why do you think it was most critical?

- What academic, thinking, and personal skills were critical to the satisfactory completion of the project? Did you already have these skills? If not, what did you do to acquire them? *(This question could be repeated for each academic subject included in the major.)*

- What products resulted from the project? Explain what you did, how you did it, and how the products you produced might be used in the workplace.

- What is one planning or decision making processes you completed while completing the project, which did not result in a physical product? Explain what you did, how you did it, and how the process would be used in the workplace relative to your career major.

- List two past or future real life career situations where you could apply what you learned. What advantage do you think you would have in those situations over another person who did not learn what you did?

A sample of an assessment plan which incorporates the items discussed above and others typically included in course evaluations is presented in section I (p. 108) of the syllabus planning form in Figure 4.9. It contains each of the three items desirable in a plan. It also includes what is to be assessed, the evaluation methods, and how each component will be weighted in producing an overall grade. The sample of the completed syllabus plan in Figure 4.10, section J (p. 113), shows how one instructor modified the assessment plan to serve her purposes.

SUMMARY

If instructors go through the planning process indicated above, using a planning form similar to that presented in Figure 4.9 (pp. 105–109), the true power of adopting career majors can be realized. The resulting career courses will focus on broad-based career clusters rather than specific occupations. They will focus on goals beyond just learning specific occupational or academic skills, and they will take into account the manner in which skills are actually applied to authentic career activities rather than learning skills in isolation. They will also take into consideration how content taught in career courses can reinforce other courses taken by students and how the other courses can reinforce the career courses. Academic courses will be taught around real applications from careers in career majors, academic courses will reinforce content taught in other academic as well as career courses, and students will be asked to reflect on how the content they are learning is relevant to their career and life visions. This will help students focus on applying what they learn to their career and life visions.

The total school curriculum will benefit from being organized around career majors relevant to students. Just as colleges and universities are organized around majors which
provide focus and flexibility to students, the high school program will be organized the same way. The incorporation of
community-based experiences within academic as well as career courses will increase the meaningfulness of what is being
taught and expand the concept of the classroom beyond the
four walls of the school.

If a school decides that it does not want to try and implement a total curriculum change around career majors, it can
modify the syllabus planning form accordingly. For example,
if each career program is to focus on skill preparation around a
specific occupation, the career scope could be limited to one
occupation. If each course is going to be taught independent of
other courses in the major, those portions of the planning process calling for teachers to get together to identify career applications of what is being taught and how they might reinforce
each other's content could be eliminated. As indicated earlier
in this chapter, adopting part of the total package may be more
reasonable in bringing about initial change. However, if the
portions that are adopted are placed within the framework of
the syllabus planning process described in this chapter, the
school will have made great strides toward reform.

Figure 4.9 Career Major Course Syllabus Planning Format

COURSE PURPOSE

A. **Course title:** _____

   (E.g., accounting, agronomy, anatomy, aqua culture, chemistry, childcare, construction, literary writing, nutrition, trigonometry, welding, word processing)

   Course description:

B. **Overall course career scope**

   This course will be part of the _____ career major(s).   *(Title of the major(s))*

   The following is a sample of specific occupations or life roles addressed within the major(s).

   1. _____
   2. _____
   3. _____
   4. _____

C. **Instructional strategy** *(Edit as necessary)*

   Students will be expected to learn to apply academic and specific technical competencies, ideas, concepts and knowledge within the context of career activities representative of those completed in the workplace. Content will be taught in an applied manner in the context of careers. In addition, academic, thinking, technical, and personal competencies addressed in other courses will be reinforced. It is expected that all students will complete and master core competencies presented in a course. In addition to completing the core competencies, students will be expected to plan and complete other optional learning activities based on their individual career interests. They will take part in a planned community-based activity relevant to their career majors. The culminating activity regarding all competencies taught, core or optional, will be to require students to apply the content to situations within their career visions. It is expected that all students will demonstrate at least minimal master level of the core competencies presented in a course.

D. Course parameters

Course length: _____

Grade level(s): _____

Prerequisites: _____

(Any requirements to enter the course)

E. Broad course goals

(Include reference to appropriate broad course goals beyond teaching the academic and/or technical content of the course. Consider school board, state, SCANS, and school-to-work goals.)

During the completion of this course students will:

1. Master the academic and/or technical content of the course. _____

2. _____

3. _____

4. _____

5. _____

6. _____

7. _____

8. _____

COURSE CONTENT

F. Specific technical or academic competencies which are the central focus of the course.

	Verb-Action	Object-Content	Career Major Applications *(For those courses in which the applications are not apparent)*
1.			
2.			
3.			
4.			
5.			
6.			
7.			
8.			
9.			
10.			
11.			
12.			
13.			
14.			
15.			
16.			
17.			
18.			
19.			
20.			

G. Career activities

This course will be organized around authentic career activities representative of the career scope of the course that require the technical or academic competencies. *(List representative career activities.)*

1. _____
2. _____
3. _____
4. _____
5. _____

H. Relevant content from other career major courses that will be reinforced.

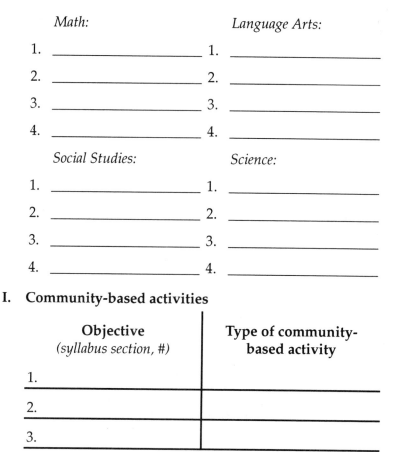

Math:

1. _____
2. _____
3. _____
4. _____

Language Arts:

1. _____
2. _____
3. _____
4. _____

Social Studies:

1. _____
2. _____
3. _____
4. _____

Science:

1. _____
2. _____
3. _____
4. _____

I. Community-based activities

Objective (syllabus section, #)	Type of community-based activity
1.	
2.	
3.	

J. Student assessment *(sample statement for editing)*

Student assessment will be based on: project completion, safe execution of workplace competencies to quality standards, group work, individual completion of project journals and portfolios, project presentations, and tests of students' knowledge of important concepts. In carrying out projects, students will be expected to be able to explain how they thought through the assignment and alternatives they considered to arrive at the final end product.

Students course grades will be based on the following:

Evaluation Criteria	Method of Evaluation	% of Course Grade
Daily participation	• attendance • class participation	15
Projects	• portfolios • written and oral presentations • checklists to judge the quality of finished products • checklists to judge the quality of project completion	25
Performance	• checklists to judge adequacy of competently performing competencies in a safe manner to quality standards • working in teams	25
Knowledge of related content	• unit tests • comprehensive exam over entire knowledge base including related academics and SCANS • written explanations of what they did and alternatives they considered • oral presentation of portfolio and practical exercises	35

FIGURE 4.10 SAMPLE CAREER MAJOR SYLLABUS PLAN

BUSINESS CAREER MAJOR
COMPUTER APPLICATIONS COURSE
(Edited with Permission of Michelle Hoeft)

DETAILED COURSE SYLLABUS PLAN

A. **Course title:**   Computer Applications

Course description: This course will address competencies in basic word processing and spreadsheet development in the context of preparing business documents.

B. **Overall course career scope**

This course will be part of a business, managerial, and sales major.

The following are samples of specific occupations or life roles that are addressed within the major.

1. Accountant
2. Data processor
3. Office administrator
4. Business manager
5. Entrepreneur

C. **Instructional philosophy**

Students will learn to apply specific technical competencies, ideas, concepts and knowledge within the context of career activities representative of those completed in the workplace. Students will be taught in an applied manner within the context of the career major. In addition, academic, thinking and personal competencies will be reinforced. It is expected that all students will complete and master core competencies presented in the course within 10 weeks. In addition to completing the core competencies, students will plan and complete other optional learning activities based on their individual career interest in order to gain exposure to business careers. Students will participate in a planned community-based experience relevant to their career interest. It is expected that all students will demonstrate at least minimal master level of the core competencies presented in this course.

D. Course parameters

Course length: one semester

Grade levels: 10, 11, 12

Prerequisites: completion of the introduction to business course

E. Broad course goals

During the completion of this course students will:

1. Master relevant technical competencies
2. Manage business resources
3. Become a productive group participant
4. Become a purposeful thinker
5. Identify a career web and develop and maintain lifework plan
6. Research a career of personal interest
7. Become a self-directed learner
8. Plan and organizes resources
9. Interpret and communicate information
10. Select technology to complete tasks

COURSE CONTENT

F. Specific technical or academic competencies, which are the central focus of the course

Specific technical competencies addressed during the completion of the major career activities will be the following:

Samples

1. Type minimum of 25 words per minute
2. Assemble materials for business reports
3. Operate a photocopy machine
4. Create a business correspondence letter

5. Design a spreadsheet
6. Create a spreadsheet
7. Synthesize information for a business report
8. Treat coworkers with respect
9. Treat equipment with care

G. Career activities

This course will be organized around authentic career activities representative of the career scope of the major, which will require the technical or academic competencies.

Samples

1. Prepare business correspondence
2. Communicate orally
3. Manage company data and records
4. Prepare business reports

H. Relevant Content from other career major courses that will be reinforced

Math
1. Calculate percentages

2. Add
3. Measure

4. Subtract

Language Arts
1. Orally communicate with coworkers

2. Write memos
3. Communicating in performance terms

4. Read directions

Social Studies
1. Social impacts of inventions
2. Cultural differences regarding interpreting events
3. Development and purposes of regulations

I. **Community-based activities**

Objective *(syllabus section, #)*	Type of community- based activity
1. E6	Shadowing
2. F2	Shadowing
3.	

J. **Student assessment**

Students will be evaluated on their ability to perform each workplace competency, the extent to which they have acquired the desired knowledge base, and their ability to integrate what they have learned and to reflect on how it might be applied in the future. In order to achieve a B or better grade, students must master the content at the minimal level expected of people in occupations in this business cluster. The amount of emphasis that will be placed on each in the course grade is as follows:

1. Process evaluations of the ability to apply competencies   30%

2. Written and oral tests on the knowledge-based   30%

3. Portfolio evaluation (end of major career performance activity)   30%

4. Class participation   10%

5

INTEGRATING AND ARTICULATING THE CURRICULUM

Integrating the curriculum means developing instruction so the content from the various courses in the major is taught in a manner that the courses support and reinforce one another. Integration can be accomplished in career major programs, Tech Prep programs, academies, or magnet schools. Often people get confused between an applied curriculum and an integrated curriculum. Typically, an integrated curriculum is applied, but an applied curriculum does not have to be integrated. An applied curriculum can be implemented by each instructor unilaterally teaching in an applied fashion. An integrated curriculum requires joint planning between instructors of courses to be integrated. The joint planning focuses on each instructor understanding what the others are teaching so that she/he can modify instruction to support the other instructors. Modifications can take a variety of forms. One form is to arrange the timing of when certain content is taught so that content from the different courses relevant to a common project is taught at the same time. Integration can also take place by instructors just referring to where what students are learning in other classes is applicable to their classes. For example, "In your _____ class you are studying _____, this is how what we are studying can be applied in those situations." The most ideal form of integration takes place around projects jointly planned by all of the instructors. The project becomes the focal point for integration. How to accomplish integration will be discussed later in this chapter.

Integration should be differentiated from articulation.

Articulation means coordinating the courses of study between different levels of education. Articulation facilitates transferring what is learned at one level of education to another. Again, career major programs, Tech Prep programs, academies, and magnet schools all have this as a common goal. Hopefully, people who complete the programs will be better prepared to enter the next level of education. In some cases, such as the magnet school examples in Chapter 2, students in high school actually take courses at a college or university while in high school. This is the ultimate in articulation because the courses taken in high school are the actual courses expected in college. However, in many cases the courses offered in high school only provide adequate preparation to enter those offered in college.

Tech Prep and school-to-work (STW) programs are examples of programs that are required to be articulated by Federal law. The high school curriculum focused on a career major is supposed to be coordinated and jointly planned with the postsecondary program with which it is affiliated. In Tech Prep, a formal articulation agreement commits the high schools and the postsecondary institution to the development of a program with a non-duplicative sequence of classes and other experiences providing for progressive student achievement leading to the development of competencies in a career major. STW programs in the high schools are also supposed to be articulated with the workplace activities.

When developing career majors, both integration and articulation are highly desirable characteristics. They take into account (a) the importance of students learning in the context of a career major, (b) the importance of students seeing how what they are learning in their various courses compliments one another, and (3) the desirability of students seeing that what they are learning in high school can prepare them to enter postsecondary institutions or apprenticeships which will help them build the additional competencies needed for life and work.

INTEGRATING THE CURRICULUM

Most integration pilot projects that are described in the literature were aimed at developing integrated instruction around one sample project or component that instructors could easily agree upon and which was relatively easily integrated. Often the pilot projects were also allocated extra funds and instructors were allocated time. Developing a totally integrated set of courses is quite a different challenge and few actually achieve it. It requires thinking through the teaching of content that is not so obviously integrated and, most often, doing so within the normal teaching schedule.

The following describes the total process that the author has found successful when developing an integrated curriculum. It is an ideal, but any movement along this process toward integration should be viewed as an accomplishment. Implementation of integration in stages is probably the most realistic goal. When starting off, those courses that instructors feel are most compatible to integration should be the target.

The integration process starts by completing the processes of identifying career major courses and developing detailed planning syllabi for each course in the major to be integrated. These processes were described in detail in Chapter 4. These processes provide the core content objectives, meaningful career applications, and the types of content taught in other major courses that might be reinforced for each course.

Once that information is available, instructors should meet to jointly review each other's syllabi. The first step is for the instructors to jointly review the content objectives of all of the courses to be integrated. Having instructors jointly review their objectives, sounds simple to those who have not done it. The author's experience with trying to integrate courses during the development of two academies indicated that, bringing instructors from various fields to understand the objectives of instructors from other fields, is quite complex. In developing both a High School Construction Academy as a school-within-a-school and a stand-alone Engineering and Manufacturing Academy, many challenges arose.

Although teachers in the same field tend to communicate well, communicating across fields is not easy. For example, social studies teachers tend to think very globally about their objectives while math and career course instructors tend to think in terms of what people need to do. Therefore, social studies teachers find it very difficult to identify 20 course objectives and to write them in terms of expected performances. On the other hand, math instructors have difficulty limiting their math learning objectives to 20. They tend to list math topics. Therefore, during initial meetings a great deal of time needs to be spent on getting all of the instructors to develop a common understanding of objectives in each field and what they mean. After that, they have common terminology to begin communicating.

Another problem is the level of planning that instructors in different fields put into their course lessons, and the expectations for those lessons. Math instructors and science instructors tend to teach from their textbooks, career course instructors tend to teach from a variety of sources and focus on completing projects. Trying to get everyone to understand that they need to teach both the theoretical underpinnings of their fields as well as to teach students processes for applying their content takes time. Once instructors understand the desirability of teaching around concrete applications, the next step is to get them to understand applications in each other's fields. For example, if the social studies instructor is to reinforce the types of applications in career courses, the social studies instructor needs to understand some of the applications that would be taught in the career course. This allows instructors to bridge between the subject matter areas. For example an instructor might say to students, "While you are doing _____ in course _____, you should think about what we are now studying. For example _____." Understanding the objectives of each of the other instructors and the types of applications of content that they are going to use allows instructors to connect what they are teaching. This allows for continual reinforcement of content between the courses to be integrated.

The next level of integration possible is to focus all of the applications within each of the classes to be integrated around common projects. For example, at the Engineering and Manufacturing Academy, the instructors decided that one project that would provide a focus for their integrated instruction would be the development of a device for the solar heating of water. The approximately 20 objectives for each course were placed on wall charts. In turn, instructors indicated which of their 20 objectives could be related to the project. The math instructor felt he could use the project to discuss the math needed to create a parabolic mirror to focus the rays of the sun. The social studies instructor felt he could use the project to discuss hygiene in underdeveloped countries and how having warm water would facilitate improving hygiene. The language arts instructor felt she could use the project to teach researching a topic and report writing. The science instructor felt he could teach the principles of heat transfer and the properties of mirrors. The career course instructor felt he could use the project to teach basic woodworking and metal working practices. Therefore, the project allowed all of the instructors to teach their own content, but around a common project.

The next level of integration possible is the just-in-time delivery of instruction around common projects. In the case of the solar heating device, the next step was to outline the order in which certain information and practices would be needed to complete the project. This provided each instructor with an indication of when the things the instructor planned to teach would be needed. This allowed instructors to internally sequence their courses to ensure students had what they needed when they needed it for the joint project.

As indicated, few curricula are ever developed to this final level of integration. The time and effort to develop such a curriculum is great. However, if such a curriculum can be developed, what most people consider to be the ideal school reform would have taken place.

In summary, the major stages of integration are:

- Identify the career majors to be offered.
- Identify the courses to be included in each career major.
- Identify those career major courses to be integrated.
- List the core content objectives for each course.
- Have instructors meet and share their core content objectives.
- Have each instructor identify the content in the other courses that he/she could reinforce.

♦ Have each instructor share the types of applications that he/she would use to teach students content in an applied fashion.

♦ Ask instructors when teaching their own applications to relate what they are teaching to the other instructors' content and applications.

♦ Develop joint projects around which to teach applications in all of the classes to be integrated.

♦ Develop a schedule for the development of the projects, which indicates when the content from each course would be needed to complete each project.

ARTICULATING THE CURRICULUM

As indicated earlier, articulating the curriculum means jointly planning a seamless, non-duplicative curriculum between levels of education. For high schools, this usually means planning with postsecondary two-year institutions. Within Tech Prep, the articulation model is founded on two years of high school and two years of post-high school education. Such a curriculum is referred to as a 2 + 2 curriculum. Having an articulated curriculum is considered important because it can allow students to efficiently transfer what they learn in high school to postsecondary institutions so they do not have to duplicate what they have already taken. The articulated curriculum also clearly shows students an educational ladder that will allow them to systematically progress toward their career and life goals.

Again, although articulation sounds simple as a concept, it is difficult to achieve. Secondary schools and postsecondary institutions have established curricula with a great deal of history and momentum. Secondary schools have tended to develop curricula to maximize a student's transfer into academic colleges. Two-year postsecondary institutions are not only looking for articulation with secondary institutions; they are also concerned about articulation with the next higher levels of postsecondary institutions. Often, meeting the requirements of the next highest institutions conflicts with meeting the requirements of high schools. Curricula where the high school, two-year postsecondary school, and four-year college articulate their programs are called 2 + 2 + 2 programs.

The ideal methodology for developing articulation agreements is for the two institutions to jointly select the career major courses that students will take in high school and in the postsecondary institution as part of an articulated program. Next, the course syllabi for those courses are examined. The objectives of each of the high school courses and postsecondary courses in the major are laid out next to each other. An agreement is reached about which content would be taught in the secondary courses and which would be taught in the postsecondary courses. Next, the instructors of courses at both levels should implement changes in their courses consistent with the agreement. When students complete the high school career major courses, they should be able to go to the postsecondary school and indicate they completed them. Students should in some way be given credit for what they took in high school. That credit could be in terms of automatically having completed the requirements for certain courses, being allowed to test out of certain parts of courses, or being allowed to fulfill related elective requirements. The goal is to, in some way, reflect advanced standing that allows students to take part in the postsecondary program in a manner that builds upon their high school courses in a non-duplicative and seamless manner.

The research literature shows that although this is a desirable goal, it is difficult to attain. Hershey, Siverberg, and Ownes (1995) profiled diverse approaches to Tech Prep in ten sites across the United States. They indicated that even though articulation agreements are a Federal requirement for these programs, they just represent plans for what is to be done but that does not mean they are being implemented. Pucel and Sundre (1999) found that little was being done at the postsecondary level to adapt curricula to the goals of Tech Prep articulation agreements. They found that postsecondary personnel felt it was the role of secondary institutions to meet the curriculum requirements of their institutions, and therefore, the responsibility for curriculum modifications was with the secondary institutions. They also found that postsecondary institutions were not identifying those who completed the secondary portions of career major programs, and students were being required to take the same curriculum as those who had not completed the secondary portions.

Articulation can be enhanced by establishing true partnerships among those who have a vested interest in the program. Partnerships are discussed in detail in Chapter 6. They often include representatives from the secondary and postsecondary institutions, teachers of the courses at both levels, academic and professional association representatives, students, community agencies and business and industry representatives, and parents. The author has found that most successful articulation agreements are natural outgrowths of mutual agreements among partners. However, most have been developed to obtain funds. Those plans often sound good but interested parties lack commitment to implement them, particularly when external funding ceases.

REFERENCES

Hershey, A., Silverberg, M., & Owens, T. (1995). *The diverse forms of tech-prep: Implementation approaches in ten local consortia*. Princeton, NJ: Mathematica Policy Research.

Pucel, D.J., & Sundre, S.K. (1999). Tech prep articulation: Is it working? *Journal of Industrial Teacher Education, 37*(1), 26–37.

6

PLANNING
COMMUNITY-BASED
EXPERIENCES AND
SCHOOL-TO-WORK

This chapter is organized into four major sections. The first presents a general overview of community-based activities. The second presents the major forms of community-based experience programs along with each of their school and community-based components and characteristics. The third presents a discussion of the partnerships that are so essential to successful programs. Each community-based type of program requires students to go into the community and to interact with people who are willing to provide them with the experiences they desire. For this to happen, schools must establish communications and partnerships with businesses and industries and other community organizations. The fourth section presents connecting activities designed to form connections between schools and the community organizations.

WHAT ARE COMMUNITY-BASED EXPERIENCES?

Community-based experiences are extensions of the learning that occur inside the school. They are based on the realization that there are things students can learn by observing and participating in real world activities outside of the school walls that support their in-school learning and provide motivation. Within this discussion, community-based learning experiences include any learning experiences within the community; including work-based and service-based experiences. Although some make a distinction between these two types of experiences, from a planning and student learning perspective they are so similar that they do not warrant being treated separately. The major difference is that service learning takes place in community service organizations versus business and industry.

School-to-work (STW) is the term applied to a highly specialized form of community-based learning that has the primary goal of developing occupational competence. Some of the specifics will be presented within the discussion of partnerships later in this chapter. STW has specific guidelines that are specified in Federal regulations contained in the School-to-Work Opportunities Act of 1994 (www.stw.ed.gov/factsht/act.htm). The act was designed to encourage state and local partnerships between business and education, so all learners could have opportunities for education, training, and high paying careers. Funding under STW is limited to those programs that involve work-based learning. Under STW, work-based learning includes any learning that occurs at an off-campus worksite where goods or services are produced.

Instructor qualifications to offer community-based experiences vary. Some forms of community-based activities that involve actual work for pay to develop occupational skills can be offered only by instructors with special licenses and with state level approval, such as cooperative work experience and youth apprenticeship. Such activities are subject to state and federal child labor laws. However, most community-based activities can be used as instructional vehicles within any course. They can be used to enhance learning where exposure to real world activities can more effectively accomplish unique learning goals or to support other learning goals. As indicated in Chapter 4, they should be identified and selected with explicit learning goals in mind as one plans a total course.

Besides being carefully selected, all community-based activities should be well planned before they are undertaken. This means that issues such as student goals, methods of evaluating the accomplishment of those goals, arrangements with community organizations, instructions to the community mentors, involvement of the parents of minor students, transportation, and liabilities must be all planned for and made explicit. Students should be required to focus their attention on specific things to be observed or questions to be answered. They should be required to complete reports of their activities. If possible, their reports should be shared in discussions with other students and the instructor. If the type of community-based experience requires a student to be in an organization on an individual basis with a mentor or supervisor, the student should be required to complete a log of activities and a summary of experiences which is reviewed, verified and signed off by the mentor or supervisor.

Planning of community-based learning experiences requires simultaneous planning of three things.

1. *In-school learning experiences*—Experiences that take place in the walls of the school.

2. *Community-based learning activities*—Experiences which take place outside of the school walls in the community.

3. *Connecting activities*—Activities undertaken between individuals in the community, and school personnel to enable students to participate in community experiences.

FORMS OF COMMUNITY-BASED EXPERIENCE PROGRAMS

There are a variety of forms of community-based experiences. Each is designed to achieve certain educational goals. They range from field trips to observe real-world activities to youth apprenticeship aimed at preparing a student for direct employment in the workforce. Establishing them requires coordinating learners' needs with opportunities within the community. The following is a list of the most widely used forms. They are presented from simplest to most complex.

- Field trips
- Interviewing
- Shadowing
- Mentoring
- Practicums
- Cooperative work experience
- Youth apprenticeship

The first five types of community-based experiences (field trips, interviewing, shadowing, mentoring, and practicums) can be offered in any course. In most states, the instructors do not need a separate license. However, instructors should clearly understand their liability and the requirements for asking students to take part in school assigned activities that require them to go into settings that are not under the direct supervision of an instructor while at the site where the activity takes place. These first five types of experiences are undertaken without pay and students are not expected to engage in the actual work of the organization providing the experiences.

Cooperative work experience and youth apprenticeship are different. Cooperative work experience programs typically require specially licensed teachers because students are engaged in actual work for pay. The same is true with youth apprenticeships. This places them under the federal and state child labor laws that are prescriptive in terms of hiring high school-age students. Cooperative work experience programs and apprenticeship programs typically need to be approved by a state agency.

Each of the forms of community-based experiences will be briefly described below. If one wishes to implement them, more complete and specific guidelines should be obtained to ensure meeting professional standards.

Field trips are an instructional method in which students take part in tours of community-based sites led by representatives of the sites. They are used to provide information on work processes and technical skill requirements of different jobs. They also provide information about what is involved in various careers and the social environment surrounding those careers. In advance of the visit, the students and the instructor should generate a list of questions and things to be observed. After the visit, students should be asked to reflect on the experiences in terms of the list of questions and assigned observations.

Interviewing is an instructional methodology where the student and the instructor develop a set of questions to be asked of individuals with expertise to answer them. The student identifies and interviews appropriate individuals, reflects on the answers, and reports the results back to the instructor who judges the results in terms of the original learning goals. The questions can vary with the nature of the subject matter and expectations of each course.

Shadowing is an instructional methodology where a student follows a person performing a certain role to learn about what they do and how. It is typically used as a career exploration activity. Job shadowing is very useful as learners explore a range of career alternatives during the selection of a career major. Job shadowing experiences should be well planned. A list of things to be observed and questions to ask are developed. They form the basis for students completing a job-shadowing journal in which they record and reflect on their shadowing experiences. Because students are minors, the selection of a site should be made with parent input. Prior to the activity, both the learner and individual providing the shadowing experience should receive an orientation as to what is expected. It is important that the shadowing experience be preceded by a letter of understanding between the school and the person who will provide the shadowing experience. The letter should include how the student will be prepared prior to the shadowing. It should also explicitly include what is expected of the individual the student is to shadow. It should include safety instruction, especially when there may be a physical risk. It should also include any information regarding child labor laws that might be appropriate.

Mentoring is an instructional methodology through which a student works alongside a person in his or her career area who is approved by a workplace employer, or an official of the organization. The student should not be expected to perform independent work or work for pay. The mentor should possess the skills and knowledge to be studied by the student.

Students should be required to fill out applications that clearly specify how the mentorships will relate to their learning goals. They should then meet with their instructors to clarify their educational goals. Based on such meetings, written career mentorship agreements should be developed that include:

- Educational goals or objectives of the mentorship.
- Expectations of the mentor and learner.
- Length of the mentorship relationship.
- Number and location of the mentorship meetings.
- Description of the mentorship evaluation process.

Once the agreement is drafted, it should be reviewed by the mentor, student, parent, and school representative in charge of mentorships. Upon approval of each party, they should sign the agreement.

Before placing students in a mentorship, both the students and the mentors should receive an orientation, including a letter similar to that described under shadowing. As part of the orientation for the mentor, students should be expected to assemble a portfolio that describes their career interests, experience, goals, and other background information to share with the mentor. Mentors should also be provided with materials that clearly define their roles and those of the student. The mentor's role should be to instruct the student, critique the student's performance, challenge the student to perform well, and work in consultation with classroom teachers.

Students should be expected to complete mentorship journals to record information relevant to their mentorship goals and to reflect on discussions with their mentors. Those journals should be organized around the previously agreed upon goals of the mentorship. Mentors should be asked to sign-off that the journals are accurate portrays of what was accomplished. The journals should be provided to the instructor. If possible, weekly meetings should be held between the instructors and students to share experiences and ensure learner follow-through.

Practicums are an instructional methodology designed to provide learners the opportunity to complete individualized projects at a community-based site. Practicums are usually short-term activities lasting only a few weeks for which the student is not paid. They go beyond mentorships in that an actual work-site project is being conducted, but not as far as cooperative work experience in which the person is actually being paid to do work for the organization. The planning process, supervisor monitoring, instructor monitoring, and parent approval are the same as for a mentorship described above. The major difference is that the student will be completing a planned project instead of completing a set of experiences while working alongside a mentor as the mentor does his or her work. In the case of practicums, the activities center on the student project and not the normal work activities of the mentor.

Cooperative work experience is an instructional methodology that offers opportunities for students to develop actual occupational skills and competencies in a paid work environment. Because cooperative work experience programs involve paid work, they are subject to a set of criteria that are more prescriptive than the types of community-based experiences discussed earlier. They are subject to state and federal child labor laws. In many states, cooperative work experience programs must be approved by the state and the instructor must be specially licensed. The work experience must meet the criteria of the Fair Labor Standards Act, which includes special provisions for 16- and 17-year-old students who are enrolled in approved cooperative work experience programs. Students can work in seven hazardous occupations that are normally prohibited for 16- and 17-year-old interns. Students must be employed under a written agreement that provides that:

- All hazardous work will be performed under the direct and close supervision of a qualified and experienced person;
- Safety instructions will be given by the school and reinforced by the employer with on the job training;
- The job training follows a schedule which reflects organized and progressive skill development; and
- The work in exempted hazardous occupations must be:
  - Incidental to the training (work itself is not the primary focus but training is);

- Intermittent and for short periods of time; and
- Under the direct and close supervision of a journeyman.

The written agreement must be signed by the employer and placement coordinator (or school principal). Copies of the agreement must be kept on file by both the school and the employer. Where the community-based methods discussed earlier can be used with any class, cooperative work experiences at the high school level can be offered in one or more of the following areas:

- ◆ Agricultural Education
- ◆ Business and Office Occupations
- ◆ Service Occupations
- ◆ Health Related Occupations
- ◆ Marketing and Distributive Education
- ◆ Trade and Industrial Technology
- ◆ Community-Based Service Occupations
- ◆ Special Needs Work Experience

The written training agreement should be developed in the same way as described under mentorships above and the training should be monitored using similar techniques.

Youth apprenticeship is an instructional methodology that establishes school-employer work-based partnerships aimed at students developing occupational skills sufficient to directly enter the workplace through a combination of school-based and work-based experiences. Once the agreement between the school and the firm or agency which will provide the work-based portion of the apprenticeship has been developed, individual students interested in becoming an apprentice apply. What is actually included in a youth apprenticeship program varies between the states. Some programs are essentially the same as the cooperative work experience programs described above. In other states, the apprenticeship leads to a certificate that a student is occupationally qualified. When programs are aimed at developing sufficient occupational competence to directly enter the labor market in an occupation, they are the most prescriptive type of community-based experience and most complex to implement. They require formal approval by the state, and a plan which integrates secondary and postsecondary in-school instruction with multiple-year on-the-job instruction provided at a worksite. Instruction should include four components: academic instruction, formal career-specific job training, exploration of the roles within the selected career, and paid work experience. Youth apprenticeship programs require a job market survey and a formal endorsement from the industry to ensure there is a need for workers. An apprenticeship is offered to students in the 11th and 12th grades and is usually articulated with higher education courses. High achievement and commitment are demanded from all of the participating students. State and federal child labor laws contain special provisions for youth apprentices. As with cooperative work experience programs, participation in seven hazardous occupations identified in the Fair Labor Standards Act is allowed under certain conditions for 16- and 17-year-old learners who participate in an approved youth apprenticeship. Upon completion of youth apprenticeships aimed at developing competence necessary for direct employment, students are issued certificates which are recognized industrywide as a mark of excellence and indicate that the youth apprentice has developed the required skills. As with cooperative work experience programs, youth apprenticeships require the approval of a state agency and they must meet a set of standards for youth apprenticeships.

Applications for establishing a youth apprenticeship program must be submitted by a joint partnership between the school and representatives from the industry and the work site in which an apprenticeship will take place. The application must typically include:

- Completion of a plan containing all of the portions of the state application form. A partnership's endorsement from the affected industry, including a local/regional labor market needs analysis.
- Specification of a plan for health and safety training.

- A plan for how school-based instruction and on-the-job training will be linked and require on-the-job multiyear experiences.
- Identification of the workplace skilled workers and/or mentors.
- Verification of the company's Workers Compensation coverage for youth apprentices.
- A marketing plan to ensure the recruitment, selection, employment, and training of youth apprentices without discrimination because of race, color, religion, national origin, or gender.
- A plan that reflects high skill work processes on which the students' performance will be evaluated based on competency-based measurements.
- A plan for how the pay for the apprentice will progress based upon satisfactory performance of on-the-job and in-school activities.
- Provisions for supportive services for youth apprentices during their training program.

For the apprenticeship to be successful, it is recommended that:

- A parent meeting is to be held for informational purposes and to include parents in the process.
- Schools provide training for the skilled workers from business or industry regarding their role as a mentor and instructor.
- An individual youth apprenticeship training agreement be signed by each apprentice, parent, educational institution representative, and employer.
- Journals be kept of the apprenticeship experiences and verified by the worksite mentor.
- A checklist of the skills developed through the internship be kept current.

♦ A Youth Apprenticeship Certificate of Accomplishment be awarded to each apprentice upon completion of the apprenticeship.

COMMUNITY-BASED PARTNERSHIPS

Partnerships are formal cooperative arrangements between schools, business and industry, labor organizations, learners, parents, and community agencies to shape and provide educational experiences for all learners so they will be better prepared as citizens and employees. From the standpoint of a school developing partnerships to enhance student learning, a partnership means any agreement between two parties to provide appropriate learning activities for students.

Under the School-to-Work Opportunities Act a local partnership has a very specific meaning. It is a local entity that is responsible for local STW Opportunities programs. It should consist of employers, representatives of local educational agencies and local postsecondary educational institutions (including representatives of area vocational schools, where applicable), local educators (i.e., teachers, counselors, administrators), representatives of labor organizations and/or nonmanagerial employee representatives, and students. The partnership may also include other entities such as employer organizations, community-based organizations, national trade associations working at local levels, industrial extension centers, rehabilitation agencies and organizations, registered apprenticeship agencies; local vocational educational entities; proprietary institutions and higher education, local government agencies, parent and teacher organizations, vocational student organizations, private industry councils, federally recognized Indian tribes, Indian organizations, Alaska Native villages, and native Hawaiian entities. The STW partnerships are designed to provide guidance to all STW efforts and not only to provide learning sites for students.

The Mohawk Valley Workforce Preparation Consortium (http://mohost.moric.org/stw/), located in the Mohawk Valley in upstate/central New York, is a school-to-work partnership that encompasses six counties. It includes 4 Boards of Cooperative Educational Services (BOCES), 52 schools districts, and 4 postsecondary institutions. Its goal is to help smooth the transition from school to work and to improve long-term employment opportunities consistent with the School-to-Work Opportunities Act (1994). The partnership emphasizes the integration of classroom instruction with work-based learning. It offers a wide range of programs, some of which are the allied health partnership program, the food industry program, the manufacturing technologies program, and the new ventures program. One STW program in the area of allied health includes the following:

- Orientation: Orientation to hospital (3 weeks)
  - Program with a focus on team building (3 weeks)

- Job Profile Module I: Business Management (4 weeks)
  - Medical Records (1 week)
  - Admissions (1 week)
  - Finance (1 week)
  - Business Office (1 week)

- Job Profile Module II: Patient Care (6 weeks)
  - Surgery (2 weeks)
  - Physical and Respiratory Therapy (2 weeks)
  - Emergency Room (1 week)
  - Medical Floor (2 days)
  - Surgical Floor (2 days)

- Job Profile Module III: Medical Science and Technology (6 weeks)
  - Radiology (2 weeks)
  - Laboratory (2 weeks)
  - Pharmacy (1 week)
  - Biomedical (2 days)
  - Social Services (2 days)

- ◆ Job Profile Module IV: Growth & Development (6 weeks)
  - Obstetrics (2 weeks)
  - Pediatrics (1 week)
  - Wee Care (1 week)
  - Geriatrics (2 weeks)
  - (OT, activities, social services, nursing)

- ◆ Job Profile Module V: Ancillary Services (3 weeks)
  - Dietary (1 week)
  - Infection Control (2 days)
  - Central Service (2 days)
  - Interviewing (1 week)

- ◆ Mini Internship (3 weeks)
  - Department that relates to students' chosen field of study.

- ◆ Presentation (1 Week)
  - Presentation Seminar (1 week)

Some of the Mohawk Valley Local Educational Partners are:

BOCES	Postsecondary	County Work Force Group Development Groups
Hamilton-Fulton-Montgomery BOCES	Fulton-Montgomery Community College	Hamilton County
Herkimer BOCES	Fulton Montgomery, Scoharie County's Private Industry Council	Madison County
Madison-Oneida BOCES	Mohawk Valley Community College	Oneida County
Oneida-Herkimer-Madison BOCES	SUNY Morrisville	

The Mohawk Valley Workforce Preparation Consortium has developed one of the most comprehensive career planning and reflection programs in the country. Students are asked to reflect on their futures and to take part in experiences verified by adults related to that future. Samples of the planning sheets from that career exploration program are presented in Figures 6.1 through 6.5 (pp. 142–148).

CONNECTING ACTIVITIES

As was indicated earlier, connecting activities are undertaken between individuals in the community and school personnel to enable students to participate in community experiences. Bringing students in contact with and arranging for community-based activities takes effort, organization, and diplomacy. Schools must generate strategies to connect school-based and community-based learning. Those strategies should include how to identify and elicit the support of potential partners. Issues such as the protocol of communications between the school and community organizations, what the learning agreements for students will look like, what the responsibilities of both parties will be, and what are the liabilities of the parties are just a number of the things that need to be spelled out. Services such as transportation and childcare need to be arranged.

After the agreements are developed, there is often a need for the professional development of school and community-site staff. The professional development activities might focus on the role of the mentor, techniques for evaluating student progress, or dealing with unforeseen events.

Due to the amount of effort it takes to establish and maintain connecting activities, many schools have found it necessary to hire specialized staff to maintain partnerships and records concerning student activities in the community. Students require educational plans before they go to the experience, mentors need an orientation to their roles, documentation of the expectations of all concerned needs to be developed for each student who will take part in an individualized activity, and there is a need to continuously monitor legal requirements. Therefore, encouraging and/or requiring community-based experiences for all students is not only a philosophical decision on the part of a school but a financial commitment.

(Figure 6.1, which appears on pages 142 through 148, consists of excerpts from the Mohawk Valley Workforce Preparation Consortium's Career Exploration System.)

FIGURE 6.1. EXCERPTS FROM THE MOHAWK VALLEY WORKFORCE PREPARATION CONSORTIUM'S CAREER EXPLORATION SYSTEM

Self Knowledge (Who Am I?)

Grade Level

_____

(Pages 1 and 2)

◆◆

1. **Assessment Results.** I completed the following assessments/inventories this year. The results are reported on page 10.
   - ____ a. Career Interest Inventory   My highest career interest area: _____
   - ____ b. Job Values Inventory   What I value most in a job: _____
   - ____ c. Learning Style Assessment   My primary learning style: _____
   - ____ d. Multiple Intelligences   My highest intelligence score is in: _____
   - ____ e. Personality Type Assessment My primary personality type is: _____
   - ____ f. Standardized Tests   I scored the highest in this subject: _____

2. **School Subjects**
   A. My best school subjects: B. Subjects in which I have difficulty:
      1._____   1. _____
      2._____   2. _____

3. **Strengths and Weaknesses**
   A. My most valuable skills: B. Skills needing improvement:
      1._____   1. _____
      2._____   2. _____

4. Two things my parents think are my greatest strengths or skills:
      1._____
      2._____

5. Two things my parents think could be improved (weaknesses):
      1._____
      2._____

____ 6. **Extracurricular Activities and Hobbies** – List your extracurricular activities (school or out-of-school) including clubs, organizations, church, sports, musical groups, hobbies on page 7. List volunteer information on page 8.

____ 7. **Honors and Awards** – List any honors or awards you received this year in either in-school or out-of-school activities on page 8. Include samples of your achievements.

____ 8. **Work Experience** – List your work experience on page 8.

____ 9. **Autobiography** – Write a one or two page autobiography about yourself – include your career interests, abilities, and aptitudes, your learning style, awards you have received, your favorite subjects in school, etc. Put a typed copy of your autobiography in this career portfolio.

Reflection on Career Decision Making

The most important things I need to remember about myself as I make career decisions: _____
_____
_____

Self Knowledge (Who Am I?)

Grade Level

_____
(Pages 1 and 2)

◆◆

1. **Career Choices** – List the two career areas that interest you the most.
   Career: _____
   Career: _____

2. **Career Research Methods** – To find out about careers, you need to use a variety of research methods. Check the career research methods you have used. Put any reports or worksheets in this career portfolio.
   ____ A. **Interviews**
       ____ Talked with my parents or relatives. They suggest: _____
       ____ Talked with my counselor or a teacher. They suggest: _____
       ____ Talked with my friends. They suggest: _____
       ____ Talked with a businessperson. He/she suggests, name: _____

   ____ B. Took part in **field trip(s)** related to careers (career tours).
       Business: ___ _____   Jobs I would like at this business: _____
                                                            _____

       Business: _____   Jobs I would like at this business: _____
                                                            _____

       Business: _____   Jobs I would like at this business: _____
                                                            _____

   ____ C. Heard **speakers** talk about careers or participated in a career day.
       Career: _____   Speaker: _____
       Is this a career that interests you? _____   Why? _____

       Career: _____   Speaker: _____
       Is this a career that interests you? _____   Why? _____

       Career: _____   Speaker: _____
       Is this a career that interests you? _____   Why? _____

       Career: _____   Speaker: _____
       Is this a career that interests you? _____   Why? _____

   ____ D. **Job shadowing** – spent a day following a parent or relative at the job site during "Take our Children to Work" Day.
       Career: _____
       Name of Person: _____
       Company Name: _____

   ____ E. **Books** or other reference materials. Two reference books I have used to research careers:
       1. _____
       2. _____

Career Exploration (Where Am I Going?)

Grade Level

_____

(Pages 3 and 4)

◆ ◆

1. **Career Choices** – List the two career areas that interest you the most.
   Career: _____
   Career: _____

2. **Career Research Methods** – To find out about careers, you need to use a variety of research methods. Check the career research methods you have used. Put any reports or worksheets in this career portfolio.
   ____ A. **Interviews**
        ____ Talked with my parents or relatives. They suggest: _____
        ____ Talked with my counselor or a teacher. They suggest: _____
        ____ Talked with my friends. They suggest: _____
        ____ Talked with a businessperson. He/she suggests, name: _____

   ____ B. Took part in **field trip(s)** related to careers (career tours).
        Business: _____ Jobs I would like at this business: _____
        _____

        Business: _____ Jobs I would like at this business: _____
        _____

        Business: _____ Jobs I would like at this business: _____
        _____

   ____ C. Heard **speakers** talk about careers or participated in a career day.
        Career: _____ Speaker: _____
        Is this a career that interests you? _____ Why? _____
        Career: _____ Speaker: _____
        Is this a career that interests you? _____ Why? _____
        Career: _____ Speaker: _____
        Is this a career that interests you? _____ Why? _____

   ____ D. **Job shadowing** – spent a day following an adult at the job site.
        Career: _____
        Name of Person: _____
        Company Name: _____

   ____ E. **Books** or other reference materials. Two reference books I have used to research careers:
        1. _____ 2. _____

   ____ F. The **Internet**. Web site addresses I have used to research careers:
        1. _____
        2. _____

Career Exploration (Where Am I Going?)

◆ ◆

1. **Career Choices** – List the two career areas that interest you the most.

   Career: _____

   Career: _____

2. **Career Research Methods** – To find out about careers, you need to use a variety of research methods. Check the career research methods you have used. Put any reports or worksheets in this career portfolio.

   ____ A. **Interviews**

       ____ Talked with my parents or relatives. They suggest: _____

       ____ Talked with my counselor or a teacher. They suggest: _____

   ____ B. Took part in **field trip(s)** related to careers (career tours).

       Business: _____   Jobs I would like at this business: _____

                                                  _____

       Business: _____   Jobs I would like at this business: _____

                                                  _____

       Business: _____   Jobs I would like at this business: _____

                                                  _____

   ____ C. Heard **speakers** talk about careers or participated in a career day.

       Career: _____   Speaker: _____

       Is this a career that interests you?_____   Why? _____

       Career: _____   Speaker: _____

       Is this a career that interests you?_____   Why? _____

   ____ D. **Job shadowing** – spent a day following an adult at the job site.

       Career: _____   Name of Person: _____

       Company Name:_____

   ____ E. **Books** or other reference materials. Two reference books I have used to research careers:

       1. _____   2. _____

   ____ F. **Letters** to business and professional organizations. A professional organization useful to my career choice:

       Name: _____

       Address: _____

   ____ G. The **Internet.** Web site addresses I have used to research careers:

       1. _____

       2. _____

   ____ H. **Career information software.** Career inventory software I have used: _____

       Results of the inventory: _____

Career Exploration Summary

◆◆

1. **Career Research Paper** – Complete a 2-3 page career research paper that includes the following sections. Put the research paper in this portfolio.
    1. Why did you select this career? (Rationale for selection)
    2. Labor market information – what is the job outlook for this career?
    3. Education and training needed for the career.
    4. List of post-secondary programs offering training for this career.
    5. Field interviews from professionals in this career.

2. **Student Resume** – Complete a typed one page resume. Put the resume in this portfolio. Resume should include the following:

Sample Resume

> **Name**
> Address (Street Address, City, State, Zip)
> Phone Number
>
> 1) **Education:**
>   Home school, major, graduation date
>
> 2) **Work Experience:**
>   Dates, name of business, duties
>
> 3) **Special Skills:**
>   Computer programs, etc.
>
> 4) **Extracurricular Activities:**
>   Clubs, hobbies, sports, etc.
>
> 5) **Volunteer Work Experience:**
>   Dates, name of business, duties
>
> 6) **References:**
>   Name, phone number, relationship to you
>   (references should not be a relative -
>   ask permission before using someone as a reference)

3. **Student Profile** – To be successful in a career, you not only need solid academic skills, but you must have well developed work skills. Ask your teachers to rate you on the following work skills so you have an idea of your ability to be successful in the workplace.

		Excellent			Poor
1.	Work Quality	4	3	2	1
2.	Attitude	4	3	2	1
3.	Teamwork	4	3	2	1
4.	Responsibility	4	3	2	1
5.	Listening (following directions)	4	3	2	1
6.	Punctuality	4	3	2	1

Career Planning
(How Will I Get There?)

◆ ◆

High School Plan. Record your plans in pencil so you can make changes. This plan should be started when you are in **8th grade.**

Grade 9

Required Courses	Credits	Grade
_____	_____	_____
_____	_____	_____
_____	_____	_____
_____	_____	_____

Elective Courses	Credits	Grade
_____	_____	_____
_____	_____	_____
_____	_____	_____

Total Credits _____

Attendance Record:
Days Absent _____ Days Tardy _____

Grade 10

Required Courses	Credits	Grade
_____	_____	_____
_____	_____	_____
_____	_____	_____
_____	_____	_____

Elective Courses	Credits	Grade
_____	_____	_____
_____	_____	_____
_____	_____	_____

Total Credits _____

Attendance Record:
Days Absent _____ Days Tardy _____

Grade 11

Required Courses	Credits	Grade
_____	_____	_____
_____	_____	_____
_____	_____	_____
_____	_____	_____

Elective Courses	Credits	Grade
_____	_____	_____
_____	_____	_____
_____	_____	_____

Total Credits _____

Attendance Record:
Days Absent _____ Days Tardy _____

Grade 12

Required Courses	Credits	Grade
_____	_____	_____
_____	_____	_____
_____	_____	_____
_____	_____	_____

Elective Courses	Credits	Grade
_____	_____	_____
_____	_____	_____
_____	_____	_____

Total Credits _____

Attendance Record:
Days Absent _____ Days Tardy _____

Career Skills Checklist

Use this checklist to keep a record of the career planning skills you develop. When you can demonstrate a specific skill, both you and an adult should initial that you have acquired the skill.

	Student	Adult
A. Self-Knowledge – Who am I?		
1. I know my career interests.	____	____
2. I know my academic strengths.	____	____
3. I know what I value in a job.	____	____
4. I can identify my primary learning styles.	____	____
5. I know my primary intelligence types.	____	____
6. I know my personality type.	____	____

	Student	Adult
B. Career Exploration – Where am I Going?		
1. I know high school graduation requirements.	____	____
2. I can identify local job opportunities.	____	____
3. I know how to investigate employment trends.	____	____
4. I can use at least four sources to find educational and career information.	____	____
5. I have completed a job shadowing experience.	____	____
6. I know the educational requirements for the careers I have selected.	____	____

	Student	Adult
C. Career Planning – How will I Get there?		
1. I have formed a high school plan (page 11).	____	____
2. I have discussed my educational plans and career plans with my parents and a counselor.	____	____
3. I am taking courses to lead to my career goals.	____	____
4. I have a post-secondary education plan (page 12).	____	____
5. I have one or more work or volunteer experiences that relate to my career goals.	____	____
6. I have developed a resume.	____	____
7. I know how to complete a job interview.	____	____

As you start putting together a resume, writing career reports, and requesting letters of reference, put the documents in this pocket. Check the reports that you put in the pocket.

_____ Resume

_____ Career Reports

_____ Reference Letters

_____ Report Cards and School Transcripts

7

EVALUATING PROGRAM EFFECTIVENESS

WHERE TO START

How is program effectiveness judged? Program effectiveness is judged in terms of achievement of expected program outcomes. Therefore, one must start the evaluation process by clarifying those expected program outcomes. Those expectations were outlined in Chapters 1 and 2. Because the role of schools within society is to educate the young to become functional members of society, the focus must be on the impact schools have on students. Throughout this book the underlying premise has been that instruction provided in the context of careers will result in students:

♦ Developing higher levels of functional academic skills.

♦ Developing general employability skills.

♦ Developing creative problem solving abilities.

♦ Having more realistic career aspirations.

♦ Having an understanding of technology related to their career majors.

♦ Possessing a sample of representative skills related to their career majors.

It is believed that developing these competencies will allow students to more effectively enter and function within a knowledge/imagination age society. It is also expected that an applied, contextual, and community-based education will increase motivation to learn and retention of students within high schools. Given these goals, the challenge is to identify measures that will be useful in determining if these goals are being achieved and to what extent. This first level of evaluation is outcome evaluation.

A second level of evaluation, process evaluation, can also be developed which assesses the effectiveness of various reform innovations in achieving the goals. As was pointed out in Chapter 2, there are a variety of school formats and innovations that are being tried in order to adapt schools to meet the new societal outcome expectations. Process evaluation provides information on the relative effectiveness of various innovations and how they might be improved.

MEASURES OF PROGRAM EFFECTIVENESS

PAST MEASURES

Since the goals of high schools have changed, it is important to change the measures that are used to judge success. Currently, a major impediment to change has been the misalignment of the measures used to determine the success of high schools and what society thinks is important. In a sense, the criteria used to evaluate high schools drive what they do. Typical measures of high school effectiveness have been standardized academic tests, occupational proficiency tests, and student retention. Academic tests such as the Scholastic Aptitude Test (SAT), the American College Testing Program (ACT), or the Iowa Basic Skills Tests have been used to determine student ability levels on academic skills. These current academic tests push for increasing students' abilities to learn isolated academic skills. Success on these tests can be achieved most efficiently by studying the academic disciplines in an abstract fashion. Efforts spent on developing skills and understandings within a career major, and creative problem solving skills are often viewed as divergences from increasing potential success on these tests.

Occupational tests, such as the National Occupational Competency Testing program (NOCTI), have been used to determine whether students have developed sufficient skills to enter skilled occupations. Past federal vocational education legislation has established additional criteria for judging the success of vocational programs. The long-standing criterion for judging whether vocational programs were performing well enough to receive federal funds was how many students went directly into the occupations for which they were prepared immediately after high school. More recently, this criterion has been changed to allow for the inclusion of those who go on for further education in a related field before employment. Success on the occupational proficiency skills tests and job placement after high school can be achieved most efficiently by focusing on the procedural aspects as well as the theoretical aspects of specific occupations. Efforts vocational students spent on developing a rigorous academic background have often been viewed as divergences from these traditional measures of success.

The past goal of retention still seems to be a reasonable goal. If students are not in school, they cannot receive any type of high school education, regardless of the innovations.

In summary, when one looks objectively at these past measures of academic and vocational program success, one can clearly see that they are keeping high school education locked in the past. As long as they are the major measures of high school program and student success, high schools are not likely to change. There will be continued rhetoric around high school reform but little action. In many cases, it is likely that recommended reforms might reduce scores on these traditional measures, which will lead to the reforms being eliminated. Therefore, some of the old measures need to be revised or removed and additional measures developed and put in place that truly reflect the expectations for the New American High School.

FUTURE MEASURES

The measures needed to realign educational practice with reform expectations can be placed into five categories:

1. Student retention and satisfaction
2. Academic skill development
3. Contextual problem solving
4. Career exploration and skill development
5. Employability skill development

In the future, a successful high school must be judged based on a combination of all of these measures.

STUDENT RETENTION AND SATISFACTION

Student retention and satisfaction with high schools are major overall barometers of their success. If students are not in schools, they cannot be educated. If the curriculum is seen as irrelevant to their needs and/or the school environment is not minimally satisfactory they will drop out or view completing high school as something to endure. In the past, people argued that if students did not want to learn what schools had to offer or conform to the school environment they should be removed in order that the schools could maintain their high standards and discipline. This makes sense if what the schools are offering are the right things and the school environment is conducive to learning those things. However, in this time of reform, the bases for judging what schools offer have changed. If schools have not changed their curricula then they are essentially trying to sell something students and society may not want to buy. In some cases the content offered is not considered relevant and in other cases it does represent the full range of competencies considered to be important. If retention is to be optimized, the curriculum must be organized in a manner that allows students to see a need for what others feel they need, or what others feel they need must be redefined. In addition, schools environments must be adjusted to allow students to be taught in ways that optimize their learning. Chapters 1 and 2 present what many feel are the current problems with schools.

Certainly, no one is saying that schools should create environments that allow students to study or do whatever they want. However, treating students as captive audiences that have no input regarding their school environment is like saying current business owners should treat employees any way they wish without concern for how that impacts the employees. Most businesses are interested in how employees view their working climates and try to accomplish their business goals within climates that take into account employee concerns. This same orientation seems appropriate for schools.

Measures of retention are readily available from school records. Typical measures are dropout rates and transfers to other schools. Measures of student satisfaction with schools vary. However, some items included in student questionnaires are:

- How up to date do you feel your instructors are with the content they are teaching?
- Do you feel what you are learning is important to your future?
- Do instructors try to show you why what they are teaching is important?
- Overall, how satisfied are you with the education you are receiving?
- If you could, would you transfer to another school?
- Do you feel people in the school care about you?
- Are you proud of your school?

Such questions could then be followed-up with open-ended questions such as:

- How might the school environment be changed to improve learning?
- How could teachers change how they are teaching to make your schooling more relevant to you?

Information gained from school satisfaction surveys could be very helpful in creating an effective learning environment. Other types of organizations have found such information useful in improving their environments. Why not school?

ACADEMIC SKILL DEVELOPMENT AND CONTEXTUAL PROBLEM SOLVING

There is an obvious need to determine the extent to which students have developed basic academic skills. Few would argue that a rigorous academic background is not important. Therefore, academic achievement tests such as the ACT and SAT will still be needed. However, in their current form they are not sufficient to assess the range of academic competencies desired of students. In the past, they worked well when the primary goal of education was to provide students with information and abstract concepts under the belief that students would be able to generalize them to situations in life and work. If educational success is now going to be judged based on successful problem solving using the content of academic disciplines in real world situations, the measures need to be expanded. Students must also be asked to show that they can apply those skills to real world life and career situations. The ultimate goal is not for students to master abstract skills, but to be able to functionally use them. The nature of the tests required is probably beyond the developmental resources of a single high school. However, school districts, states, and national agencies should recognize the need to assess these additional skills and develop or select tests that move in the direction of assessing them. If this happens, commercial test publishers will eventually incorporate these new goals into their tests.

Some academic tests have attempted to test the ability of students to functionally use academic skills through word problems. For example, some tests have a score on math reasoning. Those problems present a scenario and then ask a series of questions about the scenario that can be answered using math. Expanding the use of such items to test students' abilities to functionally apply a larger range of academic skills would be a major step forward. Currently, the proportion of such items is relatively small as compared to items concerned with facts.

CAREER EXPLORATION AND SKILL DEVELOPMENT

If one examines the goals of the New American High School, it is clear that schools should help all students develop understandings and hands-on technical competencies related to careers (see Figure 1.1, p. 9). A major goal of reformed high schools is to assist students with (a) creating visions of their career futures, (b) applying what they learn to those visions, and (c) becoming familiar with the technology and skills associated with careers. If these goals are to be achieved, then high schools must be assessed on the extent to which these goals are accomplished as well as academic goals. As was explained earlier, the criteria for making such judgements cannot be those used to assess vocational programs of the past. Most of the students in the newly envisioned career programs are not there to develop sufficient occupational skills to enter employment directly after high school. Assessing the ability of career programs to achieve the new goals requires a new set of instruments that address the extent to which students:

- Have explored careers;
- Understand the technology and kinds of skills needed in their careers; and
- Can perform a sample of technical skills within their career fields.

Because the range of possible careers and skills associated with those careers is so large, it is not feasible to develop standardized national tests to measure career exploration and skill development for each career comparable to measures of academic skills. For example, have students interested in manufacturing mastered a list of 20 manufacturing skills. Such questions may be appropriate for evaluating a specific program within a specific career area in a specific school. However, they would not be effective in evaluating the extent to which a high school has achieved broad career related goals for students across all programs.

The measures that could be used to assess and compare high schools would need to be more general. Such information can best be gathered through surveys of students as they progress through high school, just prior to graduation, and after they have been out of high school for some time. Figure 7.1 presents a sample of items that could be included in such surveys. The surveys could be in the form of rating scales where students indicate the extent on a scale from 1 to 5.

FIGURE 7.1 SAMPLE CAREER EXPLORATION
AND SKILLS DEVELOPMENT SURVEY ITEMS

1. To what extent has your high school program helped you develop a vision of your future career?

2. To what extent has your career vision changed over time? Did your high school program allow that change to take place smoothly?

3. To what extent have you explored your career area and developed relevant skills by taking part in educational activities outside the school classrooms?

4. To what extent has instruction in the school been designed to require you to reflect on how what you were learning applies to your career interest?

5. To what extent has instruction specific to your career major allowed you to develop realistic skills and understandings regarding that major?

6. To what extent have you developed a sample of occupational career skills which you feel will be easily transferred to additional education or employment in your career area?

7. To what extent did your high school program of studies help you developed a vision of your future career? What is the name of the career area?

8. To what extent did the career courses you took indicate where academic skills could be applied?

9. To what extent did the academic courses you took indicate how they were related to your career area?

10. To what extent did you participate in planned community-based experiences related to your career?

Information gathered from such measures could clearly differentiate successful from unsuccessful reform. The need for schools to show progress on such measures would clearly communicate the importance of their changing. It would change the discussion from one of rhetoric to action.

EMPLOYABILITY SKILL DEVELOPMENT

Employability skills are often considered to synonymous with the SCANS competencies described earlier. They are repeated in Figure 7.2.

FIGURE 7.2 SCANS SKILLS

♦ Three-part Foundation
  • Basic skills: Reading, writing, arithmetic/ mathematics, listening, speaking
  • Thinking skills: Thinks creatively, makes decisions, solves problems, visualizes, knows how to learn, and reasons
  • Personal Qualities: Displays responsibility, self-esteem, sociability, self-management, integrity and honesty
♦ Five Competencies
  • Resources: Identifies, organizes, plans, and allocates resources
  • Interpersonal: Works with others
  • Information: Acquires and uses information
  • Systems: Understands complex inter-relationships
  • Technology: Works with a variety of technologies

(U.S. Department of Labor, June 1991)

First, there is a three-part foundation of skills that are considered to be needed in order to carry out the five major competencies. The evaluation of the basic skills of reading, writing, arithmetic/mathematics, listening, and speaking were addressed in the discussion of academic skills above. Many of the dimensions of thinking skills associated with creative problem solving have also been addressed. The unique part of the three-part foundation is personal qualities. Evaluating personal qualities posses a major challenge to educators because there is an assumption that there is a generalized set of desirable personal qualities. The challenge is to develop assessment instruments that measure the core desired skills without violating the concern for accepting diversity. This is not an impossible task. One way of evaluating them would be with word problem tests similar to the academic application tests described above. Scenarios could be developed around such areas as interpersonal skills, honesty, integrity, and personal management, as well as others. Selecting the correct response would indicate students have developed the necessary qualities, or at least know what they should be. This technique is often used to assess employees within business and industry. Again, the development of such assessment tools can be done at a local level, but if they are going to be used compare educational programs or high schools they should be developed by professional test development organizations.

Within the five competencies listed, the assessment of the ability to work with a variety of technologies was discussed above within the discussion of the assessment of career exploration and skill development. The assessment of the ability to work with resources, information, and systems, and the ability to work with others again presents a challenge similar to the assessment of personal qualities. They could be assessed with similar techniques.

SUMMARY

The bottom line concerning the assessment of the new innovative programs is that, if the programs have additional or new goals that go beyond those of programs of the past, measures of success cannot be limited to those used in the past. Just as individual instructors are going to be held accountable for accomplishing broad goals in addition to teaching their core content, high school must also be held accountable for achieving goals that go beyond the simple mastering of subject matter. This will call for a major effort on the part of policy makers and educators to change the benchmarks for judging successful schools.